From being rescued after stepping onto the neck of a writhing copperhead to being verbally lashed by a wealthy woman over a paltry sum to gently taking the time to show an elderly man how to use his remote thereby making his life easier, this book has something for everyone. The stories are written in such a humorous, engaging style that it's difficult to tear yourself away. And the most fascinating part is that they all actually happened! Be warned that you may find yourself quite involuntarily yelling out, "Listen to this!" to the nearest person. Super interesting. Super fun. Highly recommended.

- ELIZABETH PASSO,
author of The Reindeer Gift,
The Reindeer vs E.A.Ster,
and Birthday Party SBD

The Adventures of a Real-Life Cable Guy

Dan Armstrong

ISBN: 978-1-4834-2500-9 (sc)
ISBN: 978-1-4834-2499-6 (e)

Library of Congress Control Number: 2015900821

Lulu Publishing Services rev. date: 2/2/2015

Dedication

My mother could tell stories with incredible detail.

When remembering an event that occurred decades ago, she could vividly recall aromas and sights and describe them with such accuracy that you would rather she tell you the story than experience it for yourself!

I clearly remember how much my mother loved to read and how much she loved to share her experiences.

I share the same loves. On the occasions when I would share a cable story with her, her eyes would widen and her jaw would drop. Often, she would say, "And then what happened?" Fully engaged in the tale, she would bring herself into the story as though she were standing there beside me in a customer's house.

I have a few regrets in my life. One of them is that Mom didn't get to read this book.

I dedicate it to her memory.

Our lives overlapped for a fraction of time.

You were young and vibrant.

Your future lay ahead of you, with dreams and accomplishments waiting to be taken.

I came into your life when you were twenty-eight years old.

I barely knew you, but you knew everything about me.

You picked me up when I fell, and you nursed my wounds with tireless compassion.

My fever would break and you were there.

I lay in a hospital bed after having a twelve-inch needle up my spine, and you held my hand through it all.

My speech impediment never bothered you. When others made

fun of me, you understood every word. I cried on your shoulder, and you reassured me that I would turn out just fine.

I took your friendship for granted.

I hurt your feelings, but you told me you loved me anyway.

I have not seen you for a year now.

I hope you know that I am okay.

For a second, I think I can call you. Then I realize I cannot.

Seasons have passed since we have spoken. Your last words to me were whispered, three words I needed to hear: I love you.

When we said good-bye, I did not know it would be the last time I would hear your voice.

Looking into your eyes on July 8, 2013, I could not remember how many times you carried me, or how many times you laid me down to rest.

The very next day, I wept on your chest as you left us. Not long after, I helped lower you into the earth.

I found it ironic that for all the times you laid me down, this would be the only time I laid you down.

I miss you, Mom.

Contents

Foreword

First, and for the sake of full disclosure, let me start by saying that Dan did not ask me to write the foreword to this book. I asked him to ask me. He did, and with all graciousness and humility, I accepted. I am the "other" (older, taller, and significantly less popular) Dan Armstrong—a cousin of the author.

Secondly, let me tell you how the adventure began. Many years ago, while working for a local cable television company, I heard that they were hiring installers. I notified Dan, and he quickly secured an interview. He wore his nicest suit, but since he did not own a pair of dress shoes, I loaned him mine. As with many things in life, there was a catch. My feet are two-and-a-half sizes *smaller* than his. Regardless, Dan met me at the cable office, put on my shoes, and walked into the interview. Everything was going well until he realized that all the blood in his feet was being forcibly squeezed back up into his legs. His calves began to ache and his knees swelled. Ignoring the growing discomfort, he continued with the interview. But physics and anatomy cannot be easily discounted. The soreness grew. By this point, he'd lost all feeling below the ankles. As he writhed in agony, bizarre, pain-induced thoughts raced through his mind: *My cousin has abnormally petite feet for a man. Why do I feel like a small Chinese woman? How does he walk on stumps without falling over? I love my toes; will I miss them? I can't remember my sister's name.* Fighting the ever-growing urge to cry and desperately trying to maintain consciousness, Dan completed the interview. The cable manager enthusiastically offered him a job on the spot and followed by saying,

"I appreciate your respectfulness and professionalism, but the suit was unnecessary. Blue jeans and work boots would have been fine."

Finally, to say that Dan has had an interesting career would be a definite understatement. He has worked as a professional printer, restaurant manager, drywall installer, and stand-up comedian. (He can be funny sitting down, but it's not as good.) Born with a cleft palate, Dan went on to become a songwriter and lead singer for the Christian rock band Damascus. He taught himself to speak Japanese and has visited the Far East (where he understands most of the words but none of the hand gestures) eight times. He is the husband of one and the father of four. He is a business owner, real estate investor, and master storyteller (as you're about to find out). But despite all his journeys and ventures, he returns again and again to cable television and the fascinating people he meets each day. Daniel Dean Armstrong is probably the most unique person I've ever met. I'm proud and grateful to call him my friend. Enjoy the book. I'm sure I will, once I've read it.

K. Daniel Armstrong (November 2014)

Acknowledgments

Saying thank you is no easy matter when there is a list a mile long.

I want to go back in time over three decades and thank the men who trained me in those most impressionable years. Those men were Donny Boyd, Jim Lawson, Jim Fisher, and Jeff Rickert.

A big thank you to my editor, Ken Stewart, who helped me sharpen my writing skills when I was using a dull pencil, and who walked me through this process with tenderness toward my ego.

A huge thanks to all my Facebook fans who "liked" and commented on my posts, which became the springboard for this book.

Finally, a special, heartfelt thank you to my wife, Sally. She has heard all the stories, which probably number in the thousands, and yet after years of hearing about my day, she still asks, "Any new stories today?"

Introduction

My first TV memory is of watching Neil Armstrong (no relation) walk on the moon. This glimpse of history is etched in my mind forever.

My earliest TV memories are all in black and white. Mom was so happy when Dad brought home a color TV. It was amazing! Now, on Saturday afternoons, my dad and I could watch *Wide World of Sports* in Technicolor!

By the time I was in my teens, cable TV wires stretched the length of our street. My parents decided that the three channels we got for free using an antenna were no match for what the cable company was offering for only $4.95 a month. Now we could watch twelve channels!

The choices were amazing. We had four times the number of channels to watch, and we could watch them the whole way up to midnight. The few times we stayed awake, we would hear the announcer say, "This concludes our broadcast day." Next, a United States flag would appear, waving majestically before a clear, blue sky, and the national anthem would play. Then, rainbow-colored vertical bars would fill the screen, accompanied by the most annoying high-pitched sound, as though there were a state of emergency, the screech signaling us to turn off the TV.

Today you have digital TV, Internet, and telephone through a single copper wire, and in some places, through a beam of light carried on optical fiber. You have hundreds of channels to view and to record. The video-on-demand feature allows you to access a TV show you missed, just one day later. You can record a show in one room and watch it in another.

The cable industry has grown exponentially and has taken over the phone company's market share for accessing the Web. No more hearing that annoying screeching sound you used to endure as your computer dialed up a local provider and often timed out and had to switch to an alternate number to try again. Speeding onto the information highway in a fraction of the time gave the cable company much more than a competitive edge; it buried the phone company!

When I started as a cable guy, it was just the TV we connected to. Then the VCR came out, and we had to figure out what wire went where. I remember a customer saying emphatically, "Be careful with that machine. I just paid twelve hundred dollars for that!"

Soon more channels were added, and converter boxes were created to accommodate the older TVs that only had the dial from channels 2 to 13. Sometimes, people would decline using the box because it was too confusing, even though this meant they'd have to get up change the channel. The new remote controls were just too overwhelming for some.

There was an art to tuning that old VHF dial to find the channel that was supposed to be on the specific frequency. The converter boxes made it so easy. Find channel 3 and leave it there. Then use the converter box to change channels, and voilà! Done!

I didn't grow up wanting to be a cable guy. I didn't know that was a profession. The idea of becoming an FBI agent or a police officer danced in my dreams. Maybe I'd become a truck driver, a carpenter, or even an actor, since I'd acted in school plays.

I grew up in a family that traveled during the summers and performed in churches, parks, and campgrounds. We were The Armstrong Family Singers, and we recorded an album in 1976. After I graduated from high school in 1981, I joined a band called Damascus. We recorded an album in 1984.

I loved the stage. As I looked out into crowds of hundreds and even thousands of people, I enjoyed telling stories and jokes to capture the audience's attention and bring them into my world as I saw it. Real life soon set in, and I got a real job running a printing press. Then I managed a Dairy Queen until I was twenty years old.

My cousin Karl told me there was an opening at the cable company where he worked in the office. I applied at age twenty and was hired. Five weeks of training, and I was hooked. Driving through the city, climbing poles, meeting people, solving problems—but most importantly, giving people what they wanted—was exactly what I was designed for.

I've tried other professions when cable contracts ended, and none of them ever gave me satisfaction like installing cable. I raised money for a school, hung drywall, sold cars, and even sold bathtubs. Each time I was out of the cable industry, I kept wishing for the opportunity to get back in. As fate would have it, I always ended up back in the industry and back into the homes of America.

After a long day of installing cable, I would come home and tell my wife about my crazy day. Sometimes, she would laugh or cry, and sometimes she wouldn't believe me. At parties or a get-together with friends, I would tell a story about what I deal with on a daily basis. The response was usually the same: "You need to write this down!"

That's what this book is about: three decades of walking into the homes of America and walking out knowing I did a good job, despite what may have taken place in between. I've installed cable in a million-dollar home and a five-hundred-dollar trailer in the same day, and I have learned to treat each customer with the same respect.

Throughout this book, you will meet people who perhaps you never knew existed: people who keep livestock in their basement, people who answer the door naked, people who ask questions that make your eyes roll. The lifestyles of a myriad of cultures are right next door to you, and at some time, perhaps, a cable guy stepped inside their doors and walked out alive. I've seen the shows about hoarders and laugh as I say out loud, "Hey, I think I put their cable in!"

When the movie *The Cable Guy* came out starring Jim Carrey as a psycho, I was thrilled, even though he wasn't a real cable guy. I laughed at his attempt to find the "sweet spot" on the wall to drill.

I remember knocking on a door shortly after the movie came out, and a young man answered who actually resembled the other star of the movie, Matthew Broderick. He stood back in a suspicious way, and I could read his body language loud and clear. So I said, "Were you expecting Jim Carrey?" Embarrassed, he answered, "Kind of!"

I did my best Jim Carrey laugh—but it was from *Ace Ventura*. The customer didn't seem to mind.

I have walked into the homes of the poor, the rich, hermits, the elderly, some famous people, ex-cons getting back on their feet, soldiers missing limbs, single moms and dads, and grandparents raising their grandchildren. They all have one thing in common: they all have a story. Surprisingly, they tell them to me, the cable guy.

Installing for an average of five customers a day equals twenty-five installations a week. Twenty-five installations in fifty weeks equals 1,250 installations in a year. Multiply that by thirty years, and that's 37,500 installations (or "installs," as we call them), and even that may be conservative, since sometimes I can be in eight homes a day, and some weeks will include Saturdays. That's a lot of people to meet. That's a *lot* of stories. I hope you enjoy these few I've written.

One of my trainees, Sean Brand*, exclaimed on his last day of training, "Dan! I feel like I'm in a live sitcom!"

That's a good way to describe *The Adventures of a Real-Life Cable Guy!*

**With their kind permission, I've used the real names of my cable-industry colleagues. Otherwise, the names and addresses in the book are fictitious, though the events themselves really happened.*

A Day in the Life of a Cable Guy

Moisture on the window, breath now visible, the chill air touching one's face—these all are signs of that time of year when windows stay closed at night, and blankets mean more than security.

The truck is warming up while the coffee is brewing. Add one more layer before walking out into the darkness of the day. Pull away from the house not knowing what the day will bring. No office, no desk, no computer. Just a ladder, a tool belt, a safety harness, and a clipboard.

Approaching a customer's house. Here to upgrade a certain mode of communication for them. Faster Internet or a Wi-Fi setup, a cheaper phone service through the Web, a DVR so they can record their favorite shows to watch after the kids are tucked in bed.

Second and third cups of coffee throughout the day and miles over roads now familiar.

Yup, I'm a cable guy, meeting the faces of America in their living rooms and their home offices, their spiderwebbed basements, their trailers set over muddy ground. Never knowing whom you will meet on any given day. Never knowing what problems need solving.

At the end of the day, I kick off the boots from my throbbing feet, make one last cup of joe, turn on my laptop, and use the Internet—the same one I put in other people's homes every day.

Warm Hospitality

Installing cable is a multicultural adventure. People from all the nations of the world get connected.

I remember one installation in particular, and I am reminded of this experience every time someone offers me a cup of coffee.

It was a small, one-bedroom apartment in the city. The furnishings were simple: a double bed, a crib nearby, a galley kitchen with a small table, and three chairs. The tattered couch looked like it was abandoned by the previous tenants, as did the old TV.

The man had thick, dark hair, with a mustache and beard to match. His accent was as thick as his hair. I wouldn't be there long, as this was before the days of converter boxes. Connect at the pole and screw it into the back of the TV, and it's done.

After connecting at the pole, I went into the house and started putting the wire on the TV. The excited young man asked, "Would you like some coffee? I just made some!" His offering was so genuine and I didn't want to insult him, so I agreed.

I began tuning the TV. He handed me a cup the size of a shot glass. I graciously accepted it, and his broad smile indicated we were to drink together. He nodded as he looked at me.

Simultaneously, we brought the small glasses up to our lips. It was as though we had practiced or I knew the drill. He looked out from under his bushy eyebrows to see if I was drinking when he was.

I was amused at his behavior and drank in unison with him. Here we were, two strangers from two totally different cultures, standing only feet apart and facing each other, as if we were practicing some familiar religious ritual.

I put the black liquid to my mouth and began to sip. My shock must have been obvious as my eyes squinted beyond my control. My lips pursed as though I'd bitten into a fresh lemon. His head leaned forward, and in his limited English, he asked, "Gooood?"

My tongue was spinning inside my cheeks and swirling around like a snake caught by its tail. Since this prevented me from speaking, I politely did a closed-mouth smile and nodded rapidly.

The little shot glass was half sugar. The other "half" was so thick that I thought, *This must be the actual coffee bean. He soaked it, and now it's expanding to fill the glass.* The mixture of sweet and bitter confused my taste buds. He turned to get some more for himself. I politely declined another dose of the in-your-face coffee.

Then he did something that touched my heart.

He picked up a little baby who was nestled on the couch. Like the scene from *The Lion King* when Rafiki lifts little Simba up to proudly show all the animals on the savannah, the young man stretched out his arms and presented his baby to me.

"I have come to this country to raise a family," he said with pride, "and this is my boy, my son. He is an American, just like you!"

There was silence for a moment. I didn't hear the busy street outside; I didn't hear the TV; I didn't hear anything but his words: "He is an American, just like you."

The Soap Opera

I am there to install an additional TV in the house. The woman shows me where the TV is to be connected.

Then she says, "I'll be upstairs. It's a commercial, and I don't want to miss a minute of my show."

I tell her what I have to do while she is racing back up the stairs. "Okay, I'll go get my drill and cable and ..." My voice trails off as she disappears. "Okeydoke." *Must be some great show.*

I begin running the wire from the inside to the outside. On the outside, I am pulling the wire to the length I need. When I go back inside, I see her sitting on a couch leaning forward, with her elbows on her knees, chewing her fingernails.

"Okay, the new wire has been run outside. I just have to connect it, so your cable will go off for a minute or two." I tell customers this as a courtesy.

Her head jerks toward me. She spits a nail fragment as she shrieks, "*No*! No, you can't. Not yet! Can't you wait until a commercial?"

I wasn't sure if she was serious.

"It'll only be off for a minute. I promise."

She is shaking her head while standing up in protest.

"I can't miss a minute. It's my favorite soap opera!"

Trying to be professional but also amused at her devotion to a daytime drama, I say, "Listen, if you miss a minute today and pick up the show tomorrow at the same time, I'm sure all the same characters will be standing in that same living room."

All she says is, "What?"

I acquiesce and give her a solution.

"Tell you what. When's the next commercial?"

She's bothered by the real-life question I'm asking.

"Uhhh ..."

She looks at the TV as an actor says, "But, Lilith, I love you, and I can't live without you!"

The actress responds, "I just don't know, John. What do I do about Kevin?"

The customer looks at me after the pause from both actors. "The commercial is maybe in five minutes. I don't know!"

I'm thinking, *This is ridiculous.*

I give her my suggestion. "Crack that window open. I'll go outside, and when the commercial starts, you yell out to me and I'll make my connection. It should only take a minute. Okay?"

She agrees with the plan. She walks backward to the window with her eyes and ears glued to the tube while I head out to begin my mission.

I'm standing outside under the open window. I can hear the TV show, this melodrama that's aimed at those who want to live vicariously through a phony story. I'm standing there, just waiting for permission to do my work.

I hear the crescendo of music that signals a dramatic moment in the show. And then she yells out the window, "Now! Now!"

I smile, but she can't see me. I hear the window opening farther. She is now leaning out the window and looking down at me.

"How long will this take?" she asks in a panicky voice.

"Only a minute. Don't worry; commercials take a few minutes, and I'll be done in no time." She doesn't care. All she sees is a blank screen, perhaps a reflection of her life.

"Done!" I look up. She's not there. The window is still open, but she's gone.

I walk back up the steps to the front door and enter. She is back on the couch, assuming the same fixed position.

"I'll need you to sign here."

She interrupts with a, "*Shh-shh-shh!*"

I walk over to the window. "I'll close this for you." She doesn't hear me.

I close the window, quietly walk back to the couch, and wait for a small break in the conversation between actors.

I am now whispering in a respectful tone, as if I were visiting her in a church service.

"Sign here."

Without looking up, she reaches to her right and takes the clipboard, places it on her lap, and scribbles what appears to be a name.

"Thank you. Have a great day," I say as I walk to the door. She mumbles something unintelligible.

I close the door behind me, and with a laugh, I say to myself, "These are the days of her life."

When Money Is All You Have

The house is in a high-end community. The gate at the driveway entrance opens, and I pull my van in and over the sensor that lets the occupants know I've arrived. A camera on a post swivels and points at me. I wave.

The sidewalk is textured stone with a border of polished rocks. Lion statues stand solemn watch on either side of the spacious front-door entryway.

Ringing the doorbell brings a symphony of music from within. The solid, wooden door with beveled glass opens, and the lady customer invites me in.

"Hi. Here to connect an additional TV?"

The customer is not smiling. She just says, "Follow me."

We walk up a curved flight of stairs that are at least six feet wide. From an astoundingly large window above the front door, the stairway gives a bird's-eye view of the foyer and the front yard.

Walking through the hallway is like walking down a corridor in an art museum. The walls hold framed oil paintings of foxhunts, country roads, and people in gallant poses. Every door we pass is open. Each room deserves a railing with a sign that reads "Not Open to the Public."

We finally enter the master bedroom, which could easily have won a Good Housekeeping award. The king-size bed sits under a canopy that could easily have sheltered a small crowd from the rain. The drapes at each window are layered in contrasting colors and patterns that surprisingly complement each other. Two more oil paintings of ancestors rest in tarnished, gold-colored frames.

We finally reach our destination, the bathroom. My attention goes immediately to the domed ceiling. A fresco adorns the curved space, which represents the shape of the earth.

"Here it is," she says flatly. She points to a large, marble table with a huge mirror behind it that takes up the entire wall.

In the mirror, I see the reflection of what's behind me: a tub the size of a queen-size bed, with Roman columns framing the alcove.

"You want a TV here?"

She seems impatient. "Look at the mirror. See that jack?"

I look at the mirror, and there it is. A cable jack in the mirror.

"Where does the other end of this wire go? To the basement or the attic?" I ask because I need to know where to go to activate the line.

"We paid our builder to put the wire from here to the basement. He said all you have to do is put something downstairs and it will work when we get the TV here. But we wanted it turned on before we get the TV. We have to cut the mirror to mount a shelf."

I nod as if this is quite normal. *Yes, every day I hook up outlets for TVs in bathrooms so the customer can soak up the bubbles and the news at the same time.*

"Great," I say, "show me the basement." After what seems like a twenty-minute walk, we come to a utility room that looks like a NASA control center. I am expecting to see a small desk and a chair with a spectacled geezer sitting in it, pens clamoring for space in his shirt pocket. I was happy to see that the builder had marked the cable wire with a tag that read "MB-Bthr. Mirror."

It takes me longer to walk to the bathroom, to the basement, out to my van for the splitter, and back up to the bathroom than it does to do the actual work.

Once done, I call for the customer. "I'm finished."

She is in a small library off her master bedroom. "Okay, what do I owe you?"

I look at the work order and give her the price.

"Twenty dollars!" she roars. "You're charging me twenty dollars to hook this up? That's outrageous!"

I breathe in deeply and then out slowly.

"Ma'am, it's a pittance compared to my time, the gas to get here, and the customer support that scheduled this appointment. Believe me; they lost money on this job. What did you expect to pay?"

She mutters, "It should be free with all the taxes I pay on this house."

I keep my mouth closed, but my mind is racing with things I wish I had the guts to say, like: *What do paying taxes and paying a cable guy have to do with each other?* Or *Ma'am, I just hooked up an additional TV in a five-hundred-dollar trailer, and they were happy to* only *pay twenty dollars. They just had a plumber out who charged them seventy-five dollars an hour.*

A staring contest ensues. Finally, the awkward silence ends when she turns her eyes away. *I win!*

She leads me to the office in some other wing of the house, where she writes a check for twenty dollars.

As I am leaving the house—this house with marble floors, texture-painted walls, and five-thousand-dollar chandeliers—I pause at the door and say, "Have a good day."

To which she replies, "Well, I feel like I was just robbed."

I close the massive front door behind me and walk back to my van.

Some people can have it all on the outside and nothing on the inside.

Do You Know the Color of Your House?

The description of a house on the work order is always helpful, such as: "white two-story farmhouse with red shutters at end of dirt lane," or "green Cape Cod with lighthouse in front yard."

My GPS is often wrong when the voice states, "You have arrived at your destination."

Today, the work order says "white rancher with black shutters." The GPS says I've arrived, but the house is a red-brick rancher with black shutters.

There is no mailbox or number on the house to indicate that it really is my destination, so I pass it only to find that the house numbers are going up. I realize that the work order description must have been a typo, so I turn around and pull in the driveway.

As I approach the door, I scan the work order to see the name. Before I get within knocking distance, the door opens and a woman asks, "Are you the cable guy?"

"Yes; is this 900 Waterbank Street?" She opens the door and welcomes me in.

I follow her as she shows me the two rooms I'll be working in.

A few minutes pass, and then I'm finished connecting two digital converters.

"Okay, ma'am, I'm almost done. I just have to call this in and get your signature."

She nods, and as I program the remotes, she asks, "Did I see you pass my house at first?"

I start nodding. "Yes. Yes, I did pass your house. The customer service rep that took your order wrote down that you have a white rancher with black shutters, and you actually have a red brick house with black shutters."

She looks puzzled. "No, our house is white."

Now *I'm* puzzled. "Are you Mary Stewart, and is this 900 Waterbank Street?"

She smiles. "Why, yes. You have it right."

I bring my clipboard over to her and point to the line that spells out the description of the house. "See, right there it says 'white rancher with black shutters,' and your house is brick, red brick."

She sits back in her chair. "For as long as I have lived here, I have always called it a white house."

I'm not about to argue over the color of her house or what material it's made of, so I let it go.

But I have to ask one more question. "How long have you lived here?"

She looks up at the ceiling, giving thought to the years that have passed. "We built this house forty-two years ago," she says, "when my first son was born."

I call in the serial numbers and get the okay to leave. She signs the paperwork, and I walk out to my truck.

I get in, buckle my seatbelt, and stare at a *red brick house.* I pick up the work order, and with a careful stroke of my pen, I cross out "white rancher" and write "red-brick rancher with black shutters."

The Roaches Are a *Good* Thing?

Roaches are one of the few things that make my skin crawl.

I remember walking up to a third-floor apartment in the city. I was training a new recruit that day. His name was Matt Baltozer.

As we were passing a second-floor apartment door, we both noticed a large swath of swarming roaches in the shape of a *U* just above the door. We moved to the side of the hallway as far as we could.

I noticed my trainee putting his hand on the railing. "Don't touch the railing!" I warned him.

"Why shouldn't I use the railing?" he asked as he pulled his hand quickly off the rail.

"Look at the railing. It's black. Do you think that's the natural color?" He looked down at his hands and grimaced as he noticed a slimy feeling on his palms. "What is this?"

I shook my head. "It's cooking grease, dirt from peoples' hands, germs, and it could be roach debris. When we get out to my van, you can use some sanitizer lotion to clean up."

He gasped. "That's so gross!" We plodded up a few more steps.

"Never touch the railings. You never know what germs are lurking, and you will get sick. I know because I have."

We arrived at the door of the third-floor apartment. I nodded toward the steps and whispered, "Now, if you saw that many roaches *outside* that second-floor apartment door, imagine what could be inside there!" His eyes widened.

"Matt, before we do anything else, let's go back down to my truck. There's something we need to do first."

Matt dutifully followed me without question. I opened the side door of my van and produced booties to cover our feet. As Matt was putting on the plastic slippers, I turned to get the next piece of protection.

"Okay, Matt, now take this duct tape and tape your pant legs around your ankles." Matt's eyes showed a hint of fear; nevertheless, he followed my instruction.

After we both were "protected," we made our trek back up to the third-floor apartment. Careful not to touch the railings this time, Matt followed me up the dingy stairways, purposely walking in the middle. I turned back to see Matt looking to his left and right, his eyes scanning for rogue roaches that may have left the crowd for more adventure.

We arrived at the door again and I whispered, "There's a reason why I went to this extreme care, putting booties and duct tape on." I paused. "I do it to embarrass the customer. Think about it: if we walk in like this, they have to see what we had to do to simply walk in their house."

I knocked on the door. A young lady opened it, and to our surprise, her apartment was very clean. Having made several trips up and down the steps and seeing the roaches scatter as we passed, I asked the young woman how she kept the roaches out of her apartment. She said she used some sort of bleach on the steps, but she didn't use the stairwell anyway. She used the fire escape to enter and exit her apartment.

"You mean you crawl out your window and onto the fire escape every time?"

"Yup!" she said with a smile.

"So for your groceries and everything, you crawl through the window? What about the winter? Aren't the metal steps slippery?"

"I haven't been here for a winter yet, so I guess I'll see."

I admired her bravery and yet felt sorry for her. Matt and I had to go down to my van for supplies, so I asked the young lady, "In order to keep the roaches out, would you prefer we also used the fire escape?"

It was then she noticed our pant legs duct-taped around our ankles and the blue booties on our shoes. She said, "Listen, if you have to tape your pant legs shut for fear of roaches, you better crawl out the window." We did.

When we were finished making several trips in and out the window and up and down three flights of narrow, metal steps, I asked her, "Why do you live here?"

"It's free. I sued the landlord because of the roaches, and I got a two-year lease for nothing."

"So you sued the landlord for a problem, he didn't solve it, and yet you stay here, despite all the roaches?"

"That's right. The great thing about it is, the cable costs more than my rent!"

"Hold Still, Buddy!"

It's a hot summer day.

I am driving up a gravel lane to a lonely singlewide mobile home that sits at the top of a grassy hill. I know the property is serviceable because the cable salesman is an installer, and he knew that the home could get cable.

But I don't see any options as I drive up the long, winding driveway. As I get out of my van, the customer walks out of the trailer and down two metal steps that wobble as his weight leaves them.

"How ya doin', buddy?" he asks in a southern drawl.

"Good. I'm here to install your cable, but I don't see how I'm getting it up here."

His emphatic nodding tells me he has the answer. "Let's walk over here."

We walk away from the home a few feet to look down over a beautiful, grassy field. There at the bottom stands a pole, and looking down over the slope, I can see a side road and the cable tap where I can connect.

"Awesome," I say. "A straight shot. No trees to fight, no fences. Sweet!"

We walk back to my van, and he asks if there is anything he can do. Of course, there really isn't, so I just say, "No. This is pretty standard. But I do have a question."

"What's that, buddy?"

"That house at the bottom of the hill. Are they friendly? I

mean, I'll be walking down this hill pulling a cable wire, and I didn't know if this was their property or not."

"Oh, they're fine. Old couple. They won't care."

I get my gear, put a full roll of aerial cable on my caddy, and begin walking down the hill, pulling the cable over my shoulder. This downhill trip helps me pull out the cable I need. It's always easier to pull downhill than uphill. (There's always a strategy to make my job easier.) Then I'll walk back up and mount the cable to the sub-pole. Finally, I'll drive around the hill to the side road and pull the cable up with all my might so it doesn't hang too low over the road.

The trek down the hill feels as though I am wading through water. The grass is high and thick. I'm glad I'm wearing thick jeans and tough boots.

As I get down to the bottom of the hill where the pole is, the old man from the house comes out.

"Excuse me." He is calling to me, and I want to be polite, especially if I am trespassing.

"Yes, sir. I am installing cable up there," I say, pointing to the trailer at the peak.

He nods as though he already knows it.

He says, "You walked down that hill." It is a statement, not a question.

"Yes, I did. Is that okay?"

"It's fine, but you have got to be careful." He points at the ocean of grass behind me. "That's a copperhead field."

I shudder at that bit of news. Copperhead snakes are the only poisonous snakes in our area.

"If you have to walk back up there," he says, "keep on the path you just made and you'll be all right. Just keep your eyes open."

A bit concerned but not afraid, I thank him for the advice and begin my uphill trek. As I walk, I scan the narrow swath of flattened grass ahead of me. So far, so good.

I get to the top of the hill and walk out of the tall field of grass.

I've made it. Safe. No snakes, no close calls. I breathe a deep sigh of relief.

I put my ladder up against the pole near the trailer, make my attachment, climb back down, and stow the ladder on the van. I decide to ground my connection at the base of the pole, where all the utilities meet. Grounding a cable line is meant to prevent a surge from going through the cable wire and into the house. I grab the supplies I need and walk back to the pole.

While I am standing there making the connections, the customer comes out of his trailer. He begins to walk toward me.

Suddenly, he stops.

I look over at him, and in the slowest way possible, he drawls, "*Don't ... move!*"

He is looking me dead in the eye. He backs up a few steps, reaches back with his left hand, and picks up a shovel that's leaning against a small outbuilding.

He is now moving slowly with the shovel in his hand. At this point, I don't know why he said not to move, but he says it as though I am in danger and not as if he is threatening me.

His eyes shift. He is looking at the ground. I see the direction of his gaze, and as I begin to move my head, he speaks again.

"Don't move."

I am standing on a copperhead.

The snake's eyes look straight ahead, and his tongue flicks in and out. The rest of his body is flat against the ground, stretching four feet to my left. I am frozen.

When I walked back over to the pole, the timing of my steps placed my boot directly at the back of the snake's head.

"Hold real still," the man says, and it sounds like *hold reel steel*. He raises the shovel high in the air, both hands firmly gripping the shaft like a baseball player holding a bat straight up. He is intense. I realize in a split second that he is aiming. He will be trying to drive the shovel blade straight down to sever the head that's pinned down by my boot. I'm thinking, *He's going to hit my foot, my ankle—something's going to go wrong! Oh, please, don't hit me!*

He inhales deeply, and then without warning, he thrusts the blade down fast. The shovel strikes the neck of the snake. I jump back and the reptile curls and lashes in every direction. Thrashing violently, the snake hits my leg as I am still trying to get away. The cowboy is going to town with his weapon of choice.

Have you ever had a dream where you are trying to run and your legs are twisting and you can't move fast enough? That's how it all feels. It is happening in such a slow, surreal, and frightening way.

The southern boy finishes his mission, the snake had had his last crawl, and I was about to pee my pants. I thanked him profusely for taking care of business. Had he not seen the snake under my boot, I could have taken one step or squatted down to work and gotten a real surprise.

Instead, another customer got his cable, I didn't go to the ER from a venomous snakebite, and I got another great story to tell.

An Early Christmas

She stood at the door of her apartment in her pajamas, slippers, and a jacket, sipping a coffee. I could see the steam swirling above the cup and kissing her face.

I pulled up and turned off my van.

"Hi—cable," I said as I stepped out. "Are you Susan?"

She looked over the coffee cup. "Yes. I guess you're here to install a few of those cheap boxes?" I nodded. "Show me the way."

We entered a two-bedroom first-floor apartment. It was neatly kept, and the furniture was simple, with a small TV and sparse decorations.

I sat down on her couch and began to open the cardboard boxes to assemble the kits I would be installing, and she sat across the room.

She asked if she could have the boxes for Christmas.

"Of course! They would only go in the recycling bin at the warehouse."

The door opened from the outside, and an undersized young man walked in wearing a beanie hat and a spring jacket. It was a normal November day, a bit chilly unless you were standing in direct sunlight.

"I recognize you," I said. "You work at the warehouse store here in town."

He nodded and kept walking to his bedroom.

His mother looked at him, and I saw pain in her eyes. A

concerned look came on her face, almost sad. Yet, she was smiling. "He's my baby. Twenty-one."

He came out from his bedroom. "I'll be back, Mom. Helping the maintenance guy over at 623." The door closed behind him.

She looked back at me. "He has leukemia. Born with it. His first seven years were spent in a hospital where we used to live." She had an accent, so I knew she wasn't from here.

"I'm from East Texas," she continued. "He has tumors on every joint. Treatments, bone marrow transplant ..." She paused and looked down at her cup. "I'm lucky I have him. Almost lost him several times. We had to change our lifestyle, and my husband couldn't handle it, so he left us."

I shook my head as I put batteries in the remote control. "I'm sorry to hear that."

"Well, my husband loved the outdoors, plants, pets, and with my son's condition ..." She paused for a moment. "He lived in a bubble, like a bubble boy, and it was very difficult for us. We couldn't have pets, or plants, or anything in the house that attracted germs or dust ..."

She looked over to the corner of the living room where a Christmas tree stood. Wrapped presents leaned against the wall. "That's the extent of a 'plant' that I can have."

"It looks nice," I said.

She sighed. "Yeah, well ... his birthday is November fifteenth. We don't know how long he'll have, so I put the tree up early. In fact, we put it up every year just before his birthday. I would hate for him to go before Christmas, so we have an early Christmas, and then we wait for the real Christmas Day."

I stopped what I was doing. I leaned back on the couch, put my hands together, and interlaced my fingers. She wanted to talk. She wanted to cry.

But then she smiled. "Every day I have with him is Christmas."

Please, Don't Touch My Food

The house is dirty. Well, not *smelly* dirty, just cluttered.

From the doorway leading into the kitchen from the mudroom, I can see a table with barely a space for a dish. Pieces of mail have slid from the top of a mound of unopened envelopes.

She is playing solitaire when I follow her husband in.

She yells, "I'm Sue; who are you?"

Her husband waves his hand in a "be quiet" gesture.

"I'm Dan, the cable man."

Her husband quickly takes back control of the meeting. "We want this kitchen TV set up, and then I'll show you other three."

We walk into a living room full of unmarked boxes, with stuff spilling onto a narrow path. "Here's the living room TV." He points to a large screen and continues walking.

The two bedrooms are no surprise: a trail to the bed, a dresser with a dusty TV on top. Other than the trail, there is no evidence that the carpet has ever been cleaned. My tool belt catches debris from the piles of boxes and the loose clothing clogging my path.

I look on the wall and see a familiar face in the photo of the couple. The bald man who is now brushing his whole body against me to squeeze out of the room has a full head of hair in the photo. In fact, his sideburns and hair resemble Elvis.

Beside the photo is a velvet art picture of The King himself.

"You must be an Elvis fan?" I can't help myself.

The man turns back toward me and sees me looking at the two picture frames.

"Oh, my, yes! We love Elvis!" He speaks with heightened joy. "Look all around. We have T-shirts, mugs, photographs ..." He pauses. "Everything!"

I nod, and he disappears as his wife calls him back to the kitchen.

Minutes later, I hear a loud whirring sound from the kitchen. The man is making a cake.

I finish up my work and find the two arguing over what pan to use for the cake.

"I'm finished," I announce, loudly enough to break up the fight.

Ray sneezes into his hands and wipes them on his pants. Sue looks up from the table spread with cards. "Give him something to eat, Ray!"

I've been in thousands of homes and have been offered food and drink countless times.

I've learned to be selective.

Years ago, I was offered something to drink and I accepted. The woman brought me a serving of root beer in a cup. I drank it down, and then was horrified to see scum at the bottom of the cup. So if a customer offers a drink, I always ask, "Is it in a can or a bottle?"

Ray opens the fridge and pulls out a plate with a paper towel covering the food.

"He makes the best pound cake," Sue says with pride, "and he makes it from scratch." Before I can decline, he says, "Dan, grab a paper towel there and I'll cut you a piece."

I comply. I don't want to be rude.

He removes the paper-towel covering and grabs the pound cake like it's a slab of meat and begins to slice a thin piece.

"Oh, thank you ... that's plenty for me."

He looks up and says, "Oh, no. This is just so you don't have the stale part. I'm giving you a *big* piece." I notice he hasn't washed his hands since the sneeze.

He slices a large piece for me, then picks it up and hands it to me. I grab it with the paper towel.

"Go ahead," he says, "eat it." Both he and his wife stare at me.

I have to make a quick decision. Not wanting to offend them, I break the pound cake in half below the place where his bare hands touched the food—the food I am about to put into my mouth.

I take a mouse-nibble bite. "Mmmm, that *is* good."

Ray speaks up. "You didn't even take a bite!"

I have to think on my feet. "Oh, but Ray, I did! If I take a big bite, my taste buds will be overwhelmed, but if I take a little bite, like sipping wine, I get the true flavor."

They buy it.

"I'll finish the rest at home. Besides, Ray, *my* hands are dirty!"

A Reminder of My Blessings

An old man in a wheelchair meets me at the security door of a low-income housing building.

Immediately, he is confrontational. “I don’t know why you’re here! My daughter set this up to save me money, and all you’re going to do is pick my pocket! All you do is show reruns, and I’m sick of this. You can shove this cable up your a&$.”

My eyebrows are instinctively raised by his less-than-cordial greeting. Typically, I am met with a grand welcome. After all, they’ve made a call to improve their service or add a product that interests them, but this man would have none of that.

Time to turn on the charm. “Mr. Smith, I understand your frustration. I’m here to swap out some equipment to save you money. Isn’t that why I’m here?”

He doesn’t answer the question. “You’re like the Mafia. Once they got ya, they got ya!”

I purposely conceal my chuckle. “Mr. Smith, do you want to cancel this appointment and keep paying the higher bill or let me do my work and lower your bill?”

I can tell he has no choice. “Fine, follow me.” He turns his chair, and we roll into the elevator. He is still grumbling as we make the ascent to the third floor.

We travel down the hallway to his door and into the efficiency apartment. A bed in the corner, a couch and chair, and a small kitchenette are all there is to it. It’s more like a hotel room than a place to call home.

He moves from his wheelchair to a lounge chair. "My remote doesn't work for the TV, so I roll up to the TV every time and change the channels." He is raising his voice again. "I'm not buying a new TV, so this better work!"

"Sir, when I am finished, the new remote I provide you will turn the TV on and off and change the channels so you can stay in your chair."

He nods and settles down.

I finish programming the remote, then kneel down beside him and place the remote in his hand.

I have not realized how blind he is. When I point to the on/off button, he brings the remote up so close to his face that his finger can barely fit between his "good" eye and the remote.

"Where is it?" he says in an agitated tone.

Using my index finger and thumb, I pinch his bony finger and move it over to the button. "It's right here at the top left of the remote," I say in a calm voice.

Keeping my pinch, I pull him down to the channel and volume buttons. "Volume is here on the left, and the channel button is here on the right. You can feel them and see that they are like toggle switches."

The remote is almost touching his face as he moves his finger from left to right several times to orient himself to the new device.

"Okay," he says, "I think I have it."

I stand up by his side and ask him if he wants me to sign the work order. He begins to spell his name even though I can clearly see it printed at the top of the work order.

"Okay, sir, I'll leave your copy here on the table. Have a good day."

He is still experimenting with the remote, turning the volume up and changing channels. "Okay, sonny ... you have a good day, too."

I walk the three steps to the door and hear him say, "Thank you for coming by today. I guess this wasn't a bad idea after all."

I turn back and respond, “Well, thank your daughter. She was just trying to save you money.”

He turns to look over his shoulder. “Yes, but you made it easier to watch TV.”

Closing his door and walking down the hallway, I am very grateful for my eyes, my legs, and the place I call home.

Two Hundred Chickens

It was a cold October day.

I was there to install a TV in the living room of a ranch-style house. The woman showed me where the TV would go.

I explained that I would need to drill down into the basement and then from the basement to the outside of the house. "Where's the door for the basement?" I asked.

"Oh, it's over here," she said, motioning toward the kitchen. "But I must warn you: there's two hundred chickens down there."

Never heard that one!

"Really?"

"Yes. It was cold outside last night, and we brought them in."

I moved the towel that was rolled up at the bottom of the door and pulled the door open slowly.

The smell of ammonia shot up my nose, and my eyes started to water. "You're not kidding!" I said.

As I descended the steps, I heard the cackling. Then I walked through the horde of hens, and they separated like I was Moses parting the sea.

I geared up with a hammer drill to bore through the block wall to make room for the new cable wire. *Rooooarrr!* My drill rumbled through the structure.

As I was drilling, I thought, *I wonder what these chickens are thinking?* Yes, I thought that!

The sound of the drill filled my ears. Then I released the trigger.

To my surprise, the basement was dead quiet. I turned around to see two hundred chickens silently staring at me.

Suddenly, one solitary hen stretched her neck above the rest and shrieked, "Ba-*gock!*" Then another one, then another.

I pressed the trigger for the fun of it, and again, all heads went down. Again, they went motionless and stared at me.

I could almost hear them thinking, *We weren't talking to you.*

I Really Don't Need to Know

Entering a house to install cable service is what I do.

But, in addition to being a cable guy, I am also a counselor, an interior-decorating consultant, and a computer technician, and today, I become a party to strange confessions.

"Hi, I'm Dan. Here to install your cable."

The man lets me in and points to the TV across from the couch, where a woman sits tapping on her computer.

"We're not married!" she announces.

I had already knelt down to tune the TV. Still on my knees, I turn to look at her.

She nods toward two Cheerio-eating boys on booster seats at the table. "Those two boys are not ours. They have light hair and we have dark hair. They are not his and they are not mine." She says it emphatically. "I am only here to do my laundry and use his Internet."

Now I'm shrugging my shoulders. A lot. "Okay," I say with a smile, "I'm just here to give you cable."

The man is picking up small bits of cereal off the floor. "I'm babysitting for a friend of mine while she's at work, and this is Michelle, my neighbor. She comes over to hoard my Wi-Fi and use my washer." He says it in a teasing tone.

She begins to defend herself. "I'm only here on Wednesdays and Saturdays." Then she looks at me and says, "There's nothing going on!"

Now keep in mind, I *had not* asked *one* question! They must think *I* am thinking, *Here's a young couple with two children.*

She closes her laptop and says to the man, "I'll be back in an hour to get my wash." She leaves, and the man closes the door behind her.

He snorts and says, "This is a nosy neighborhood. There's a rumor going around that her and I have something going on, but really there isn't."

I am befuddled. *Why do they feel the need to clarify this to me, a complete stranger?* So I ask, "Why do think you need to tell me all this? I'm just here to install your cable."

He rolls his eyes. "I guess she's afraid you'll be at someone else's house in here today, and she's just tired of the talk."

I chuckle. "Don't worry. You're the only appointment I have in this neighborhood today."

He grimaces and runs his hand through his hair. "Well, there's really nothing going on."

I look him dead in the eyes and say, "Dude, I believe you, okay? I'm just here to hook up your cable, that's it."

He sighs. "Okay, the other TV is back here in the bedroom."

I'm tempted to play into his fear of being misunderstood. I want to ask him, "Does your girlfriend have a specific place in mind?"

I didn't, but oh, how I wish I did!

"I Sure Do Miss Her"

Sometimes I wonder why people are so open to a stranger.

I knock on the door of the apartment.

A woman who appears to be in her sixties opens the door.

"Hi, I'm Dan, from the cable company. Here to exchange some equipment for you?"

I state who I am, but I end with the question to prompt the customer in dialogue about why I am standing at their door.

"Yes," she replies, "I don't need this recorder anymore, just something basic."

She moves aside so I can walk past her into her tiny, one-bedroom apartment. The big- screen TV is only six feet from the couch and takes up nearly half the room.

"We're doing this TV and one in the bedroom, right?"

"Yes." She plops down on the couch as she's pointing. "Can you get behind that monster?"

"Oh, yeah," I say. "No problem."

We are sixty seconds into our first meeting when she asks, "How do you like my flowers?"

I peer over the top of the TV and see five pots of fresh flowers, with plastic stems holding small cards.

"They're beautiful." I pause to look at all of them and then squat down again.

"They are from my sister's funeral. She died last week from a massive heart attack. I sure do miss her."

I stop what I'm doing. I'm not quite done behind the TV, but

I stand up so she can see me. I look at her solemn face. "I am so sorry. How old was she?"

She looks down at the flowers sitting between the TV and the couch. "She was fifty-*one*." She emphasizes the *one*, as though she is angry. "Her husband says she always snores, and he woke up because he didn't hear her snoring. He turned on the light and her lips were blue."

Her eyes start to fill with tears. "He always made a joke about her snoring and how it kept him up at night, but now he says he can't sleep because he doesn't hear her snoring."

I nod and pause for a few moments before disappearing behind the TV again.

"She was so young," I say as I hook up the equipment.

It's quiet for a minute. I stand up and come out to the space in front of the couch. "I am going to program the remote so you only need one. It will operate your cable box and your TV."

I'm not sure what else to say.

I have another motivation for not engaging too much. Two guys have called off today and all their appointments have to be covered, which means there will be little time to socialize throughout the day. I am in a hurry.

But for this installation, I realize I have to slow down.

"Let's hook up the one in the bedroom," I say as I gesture toward the door.

She pushes herself off the couch with a grunt and follows my lead. After installing the box and programming the remote, I say, "Okay, they're both done."

She's not interested in the new remote. She wants to talk. "I'm not that old, but she was so much younger than me."

I look down at my clipboard and pen. It's not a good time to ask her to sign it. An awkward silence grows as I stand there and wait for her to speak again.

"Are you going to be okay?" I ask, but in all honesty, I really want to leave. The extra appointments I have taken on mean I have to be efficient, not only in doing the work but also in explaining the services quickly and moving on.

It's quiet again. She's looking down with a blank stare. "I'll be all right. Thanks for asking." She turns and walks out to the living room and sits down on the couch. It's a good time to ask for her signature. She signs the order, and I hand her the copy.

"Take care of yourself," I say.

She nods and reaches up to shake my hand. I usually say "Have a good day" when I leave, but it seems inappropriate here.

Instead, I say, "Thanks for sharing your flowers with me."

She smiles, then looks down at the flowers and back at me. "You're welcome."

Tip Not Needed

You never expect it, but when a customer hands you a monetary tip, it's much appreciated.

He is an older man who has just moved in with his "kids," as he puts it. The basement "living room" has no carpet. The bedroom is walled off and private, at least.

I notice no windows. Understanding building codes, I know this is a violation. It's a fire hazard when there's no exit from a bedroom except the primary door. I ask if he keeps the door open at night. He says he does because it gets too hot.

I'm hooking up the digital box to a TV, and I am far behind schedule. Earlier installations have required more work than was scheduled for.

Then he asks, "While you're here ..."

When you hear that phrase, you know you're about to be asked a "favor" that may take extra time that was not allotted for this particular appointment.

"While you're here, could you hook up all that equipment?"

It's a VCR/DVD combo unit, a Blu-Ray player, and a Wii game console. He continues, "My grandson won't be home for a while, and I always seem to be bothering him. My eyes are bad, and I don't know what wires go where."

I sigh, making sure he doesn't hear me. I really don't want to do it, because it means I have to test all the connections as well, which will put me further behind in my day.

Then I say, "Sure."

I crawl behind the TV, using the flashlight feature on my phone to see. A jumble of wires lies in a pile. One by one, I connect the audio and video jacks and the coaxial cable.

"There, it's done," I say. I also know he's not going to get it until I explain what input is what. So I say, "Grab your remote."

He picks it up and stares at it. I continue, "Okay, see that button that says 'input'?" He looks down at the remote cradled in his hand and scowls. "Uhhh, oh, yes ... I see it."

"Good. Now press it, and you'll see a selection of inputs to choose from." He presses the button on the remote and the menu of choices shows up on the TV.

"Using the arrows, you can scroll down and pick the input to use the device you want to activate." He nods, looks at the screen and then up at me like a lost puppy.

I see his problem. He doesn't know which input operates which device.

"Tell ya what. Let me write down a guide for you."

I grab my pen and write:

Inputs:
HDMI is for cable
ANT is for VCR/DVD
Video input 1 is for Blu-Ray player
Video input 2 is for the Wii

He plays with it for a minute. He gets it!

"It looks like you know how to use it, right?" I say. He nods, this time with confidence.

I ask him to sign my work order. Then I begin to walk away, saying my usual line, "Have a good day."

He shuffles behind me to the door, taps me on the shoulder, and extends his hand for a shake. In it is a ten-dollar bill.

"Sir, you don't have to do that!" I exclaim.

To which he responds, "No, but neither did you."

Oops!

Addresses can be confusing.

Ninety-five percent of the time, a printed work order has the correct information to help me locate the house. The color of the house; a landmark on their property, such as a flagpole in the front yard; a white fence around the house; a sign for a hair stylist; or a two-car detached garage—they are all helpful hints.

In the city, however, most of the houses look the same.

I have an order for a house on West Chestnut Street. I know the city pretty well and rarely use a map or GPS. Knowing where to turn on one-way streets to end up in the right block is a skill I learned from many years of navigating the city.

I pull up in front of the house. I look at my work order, then up at the front door. The numbers match.

I knock on the door and a man answers.

"Yes?"

"I'm Dan. Here to install your cable."

He thinks for a moment, then invites me in. "My wife must have ordered this. I didn't know you were coming. We talked about it, so I guess she went ahead and made the appointment." I am nodding.

"Yeah, I hear that a lot. Am I hooking the one up in the living room?" I see a TV near a bookshelf. He looks over at it and says, "Yes. We only have one TV. We read a lot and I don't watch too much, but it would be good to see the news once in a while."

I look around for the best way to get a wire to the TV. I explain that since the house has never had cable run to it, I would be outside for a while getting a line from the pole to the house. He agrees to our plan, and I get busy.

About an hour later, after fighting tree branches and other wires, I get the new cable service to the house. I go inside to complete the rest of the installation.

Twenty minutes later, the TV is on and the man is smiling.

"Wow, that is a good picture. I'm glad we got this done."

Just then, the front door opens and his wife walks in.

"Hi, Honey," she says. Then she sees me. "Hello. Who are you?"

I've heard this question before, but this time, it seems a little strange.

"My name is Dan. I just finished installing your cable." She looks at her husband, who is standing to my left. "Oh, so you decided to get the cable?"

He frowns, almost out loud. "No. I thought you did."

I look to my left at the man, then back at her. One of these people made the appointment, and neither of them is going to take the credit or the blame.

My only saving grace would be the work order. It will have their name and address clearly printed. It will prove that someone ordered the cable.

"My work order has the name of ..." I pause, almost dramatically, to reveal the culprit. " ... Henry Shepherd." I grin and look at the man with my eyebrows raised as if to say, *So, you were the one!*

His head jerks back. I'm ready for his wife to chastise him, and I'm feeling like it's time to go before she lets him have it.

Strangely, she isn't looking at him. She is staring at me from under arched brows.

He speaks up and breaks the awkward silence. "My name isn't Henry Shepherd. What's that address on your work order?"

I'm confused. I look down at my work order and read aloud, "Henry Shepherd, 545 West Chestnut Street." I look up for validation, but there is none.

The lady walks away without a word. The man, who I'd thought was kidding around, is humorless. "My name is Roger Ball, and this is 545 West Walnut Street."

My jaw drops and my heart skips a beat. All the time I was there, I thought this man's name was Henry. He *looked* like a Henry. But now ... now he is Roger.

Finally, I announce the obvious. "This is awkward."

I look down at the work order again. Maybe there's a chance he's making a mistake.

But he's right. He is Roger Ball. I'm at the wrong address and didn't think to ask for his name at the door. Now what?

I am a little embarrassed, but then I let out a sigh, smile, and ask, "So, do you want the cable to stay on?"

He smiles too. "No. You'd better turn it off. My wife and I have to talk about this."

I find Henry Shepherd's house. When he answers his door, I ask, "Are you Henry Shepherd?"

He opens the door wide. "Yes! I've been waiting all day for you."

"I would have been here sooner, but I had some trouble at my last appointment."

Something You Just Don't Ask the Cable Guy

After hooking up Internet wireless service in the couple's office, I move to the kitchen, where the woman has a laptop, a Kindle, and an iPad for me to configure. She also has a Sirius radio connected to a Bose system.

The husband is sitting at the table eating a sandwich, spitting as he says, "This better all work!"

I laugh and say with a smile, "That's why I'm here."

While I type in passwords on all the wireless devices, he asks how long I've been doing cable.

"Well, I started when I was twenty, and I'm now fifty."

He nods and takes another bite. "Do you remember the old TVs with the UHF and VHF dials on them?"

I'm spinning a dial on the Sirius radio to input the password. "Oh, yes. I used to have to turn the dials until the twelve channels came in. I am so glad we don't see them anymore."

He chews some more. "I'm retired now. I used to drive truck for a living. I'm almost twenty years older than you."

I look directly at him and see the thick, gray hair on top.

"Wow ... almost seventy and you still have a full head of hair!"

Suddenly, his wife joins in. "He is so lucky."

He shakes his head. "No, no. I wish I were bald. It's so much trouble with all this hair."

I laugh. "That's funny; I wish I *had* that much hair!"

His wife pipes in again and asks me, "Do you have hair on your chest?"

My eyes bug out.

The man throws his hands up in the air. "Whoa! Whoa, woman!"

She begins to clarify. "You know, when men have a full head of hair, they don't have any on their chest, and when men are bald, the hair shows up on their chest."

At this point, I'm not sure what to do. Despite her reasoning, I'm not about to rip my shirt off to prove anything.

The Sirius radio finds the signal and I say, "There it is. It found your network, and I can find the door."

Who Ordered the Cable?

Time frames for installations are printed on the work order: 8:00 a.m. to noon, 10:00 a.m. to 2:00 p.m., and noon to 4:00 p.m. This gives you enough time to arrive, complete the work, and explain the services.

Often, I arrive at 11:00 a.m. for the morning appointment, due to other morning installations. As long as you arrive within the time frame, it is accepted as being on time.

I arrive at the address at 9:00 a.m. The man opens the door and immediately asks, "How long is this going to take?"

Now, I know I have until noon, and the house already had cable run to it in the past, so I reply, "That depends. Are all the wires where you want them?"

He looks over my shoulder and then at his watch. "Umm, yeah ..." He hesitates. "I do need one in my basement."

I nod and ask him to show me around. We walk to the rooms and then the basement where he wants cable installed.

I'm pretty good at estimating how long the install will take, so I give him my best guess. "This will take me about forty-five minutes, give or take. Are you in a hurry? Do you have to go somewhere?"

He shakes his head. "No."

I am confused by his body language and his hurried demeanor—looking at his watch, looking out the windows as I begin working, asking how long it will take.

I get to work. I bring my cable caddy and cable roll in the house and drill the hole necessary for the basement wire, which has to be stapled to the ceiling joists.

Then I hear a door slam. An argument ensues. The wife is calling her husband an idiot. I'm in the basement, but I can hear every word.

I walk up the steps and out the door to my van to get my staple gun. As I'm loading the staple gun, I hear a loud crash of metal. It's my cable caddy being thrown out the door! I can't believe what I'm seeing.

Then I see the wife throw my clipboard. As it's flying through the air, the papers come loose and become little kites drifting down to the yard.

I'm stunned. *What happened in that house?*

I walk up to the front door and knock. Anyone outside could hear the foul language and angry exchange. I dare not just walk in.

The man answers. "Sorry about that. I ordered the cable, but my wife didn't want it. I guess we have to cancel this today." *That's* why he's behaving suspiciously. He wanted it done before she got home.

Then I hear her shouting at the top of her lungs, "You better not walk in this house again!"

I know she's talking to me, because he doesn't turn his head to look at her.

I lose my cool. "Lady, you just threw *my* equipment out the door. If anything is damaged, *you* are paying for it. My paperwork is all over the yard. And I *need my drill*!"

She disappears. "I'll go get it," the man says.

He returns while I'm hauling my cable and caddy back to my van. He hands me my drill and says, "I'll help you get all your papers."

I shake my head and say, "So, I guess we both know who wears the pants in this house."

He cocks his head back in surprise, but I don't care. He put me in a bad situation, and her behavior was unnecessary. I rarely raise my voice to a customer, but I knew that was the only way she knew how to communicate.

For quite a while after that, I would ask, “Does your husband or wife know we’re installing cable today?”

Nosy Neighbors

It happens. I'm up a pole hooking up cable when the neighbor comes out and asks, "May I help you?"

I know they are not really offering assistance. What they are asking is, "What are you doing?"

It's really none of their business. By law, I'm not allowed to discuss what I'm doing at their neighbor's house. To disclose information would be a violation of the Privacy Act. Do *you* want your neighbor knowing you're getting cable?

So I usually just remain quiet and act as if I didn't hear them. The fact is, I am working twenty feet in the air, and I have to focus on what I'm doing, not turn to face them and answer a question.

If they ask again, then I just say, "I'm working on the cable."

This woman isn't satisfied with my first two responses. She allows her door to close behind her and takes a few steps away from her house. Shielding her eyes from the sun with her hand, she calls out, "I want to know what you're doing! You could be a terrorist for all I know!"

I let out a sigh but remain busy.

She calls out again. "I'm calling the police!"

I wrap up what I need to do and unstrap myself from the pole. As I'm climbing down, I notice she hasn't moved. She's not going away.

I decide to be firm but professional. "Ma'am, I am working on the cable for someone else. I am not allowed to tell you whose cable I am working on because it would be a violation of the Privacy

Act. And besides, ma'am, I am not on your property, and I am not working on your cable."

I thought that would appease her. I was wrong.

"How do I know you're not putting a camera up there? I want to see your identification."

I know these types. This isn't the first time I've run into them. They are the busybodies of the neighborhood. They are the kind of people who count the cars in people's driveways and later ask them who was visiting. They sit and stare out their window, looking for "outsiders."

I'm at the bottom of the ladder now. I lower it and place it on my shoulder.

Now the husband comes out. He walks up beside his wife and asks, "May I help you?"

Seriously! Instead of losing my temper, I decide to answer the question exactly as they asked it. "No, I don't need any help. I pretty much know what I'm doing."

I turn toward the house I'm working on and begin walking up the yard.

The couple seems shocked that I answered the exact question they asked instead of the real question they were asking.

The man speaks up. "Sir, I'm going to write down your license plate number and call the police." It was a statement, not a question, so I didn't feel obligated to answer.

"Did you hear me, young man?" I notice I've gone from "sir" to "young man," which is an obvious indication of his attempt to lower my stature in his eyes.

He's asked a question, and it needs a response. My typical response, "I'm working on the cable," is usually satisfactory. But this couple wanted way more than company policy allowed me to give.

Did I hear him? Yes. But walking uphill with a twenty-eight-foot extension ladder that weighs eighty pounds is not easy, so instead of turning my ladder and stopping mid-stride to address his question, I turn my head and raise my voice. "Sir, I am working on the cable. It has nothing to do with you. Call the police, please, because I would like to file a complaint against you. I don't have their number, so you would be doing me a huge favor."

It is rare that I speak with anything but courtesy, but once in a while, the bulldog comes out of me. Perhaps had I given them the information up front and not protected the privacy of their neighbors, I would not have incited their fury. But truly, it was none of their business.

I once heard it said that mean and nasty people are only 1 percent of the population.

The problem is, they move around a lot.

No Sweat!

Summer is my favorite time of year: hot temperatures, long days, cold drinks offered by the customers, and driving with the window down. I could be a dog.

The man who answers the door smiles broadly and greets me enthusiastically.

He's wearing a sweaty, brown T-shirt. His hair flap is sticking to his bald head except for a few lost strands hanging over his left eye. His big, bushy eyebrows and his bold mustache are both encroaching on his face with careless abandon. His beard is short with gray specks and doesn't match the ferret resting under his nose.

His belly hangs below his T-shirt, which looks two sizes too small. He reminds me of Homer Simpson, only with facial hair.

He is perspiring heavily and explains why the moment he opens the door. He stammers, out of breath, "I just got done mowing the backyard," *pant*, "and I just happened to see you pull in my driveway."

He steps back as I walk in, looking at my clipboard.

"You're here to hook up my Internet, and I must apologize, but my air conditioner is not working."

I smile. "It's okay, I don't mind the heat. Where's your computer?"

He points down the hallway. "Do you mind if I watch you?"

I start toward the dark hallway. "No, I don't mind. I actually like it when people do. That way, I don't have to explain what I did when I'm finished."

"Oh, good. I don't want to be a bother!" He's jovial, despite his soaked attire.

I stop at the end of the hallway, a door on either side. "Which door is it?" I ask.

"It's the one on the right," he says with a broad smile.

I reach for the doorknob. "It's locked, sir."

I hear keys jingling as he reaches in his pocket. "Oh, I forgot. I lock this up when my grandkids come by so they don't mess with my stuff."

Before I have a chance to move, he squirms between me and the locked door. His arms, coated with a mat of wet hair, rub against my right arm. His sweaty mass smears me like a corncob being slathered with butter. I feel like I've been slimed. I shudder, feeling totally disgusted.

The door opens, and he leads me into a tiny, cluttered room. I see what I need to do and go about getting a cable wire into the room from outside.

A few minutes later, I'm back in his office. We pull his desk from the wall so I can connect an Ethernet wire from the modem to his PC. The room is dark. There are no overhead lights, so he offers me his flashlight so I can see what I'm doing.

It's a tight space. I have to lie on my side and reach around the back of his computer. I reach up from the floor to take his flashlight, but he insists on helping.

"I'll hold it for you," he says. "I want to see where you're hooking it up in case I have to change anything." He turns it on, and I turn my head to avoid being temporarily blinded.

I scoot myself as close as I can, and with the Ethernet wire in hand, I reach behind the heavy desk. He leans over me and points the flashlight down.

Then I feel something on my neck. It's a drip of water. My head twitches. I reach and feel for the connection on the back of the computer. I feel it again, only this time it's two drips on the back of my neck. I find the port and feel the wire click into place.

I feel it again.

I turn to look up at the man shining his light in my direction.

I see the source. It's his sweat.

He is dripping on me, and I am helpless.

I see it coming, and I can't possibly escape. A droplet of water is leaving his forehead. Everything goes into slow motion. I am lying on my side in a tight space between a wall and desk. The bead of sweat is joining forces with all the other drops spilling out of his pores.

I just can't move fast enough. The flashlight, still beaming, is casting a shadow on his face, but it's also highlighting the liquid as it builds momentum.

It grows larger and larger as it crawls down his cheek.

Gravity has its way, and it leaps off his flesh and falls toward my face.

Somehow, in the nick of time, I pull my body back. I see the deluge hit the thin carpet in front of me and absorb into the fibers.

Real time finds me standing up, wondering how I got out of such a small space in record time.

I wipe the back of my neck with my hand and shudder again, knowing this man's sweat has made contact.

"May I use your bathroom?" I ask quickly.

"Sure. I'll show you where it is."

He wobbles to the door. "Here it is!"

I walk in quickly, only to find used towels hanging over the shower-curtain rod. I wash my hands and then wash my neck with my bare hands. I'm not going to use any of those towels, either.

I walk out the door, and the man sees I'm wet around my collar.

"Do you need a towel? I can get you a towel."

I shake my head. "No, that's okay. I just needed to cool off, just needed to get some *fresh* water around my neck."

He smiles. "Yeah, nothing like a cool washcloth on a hot day."

I nod. "Yeah ... I'd rather have that than a *sweaty neck*."

You Just Do What You Have to Do

Decades later, I am still haunted by the sight.

I am twenty-one years old, and I'm twenty feet up, standing on a ladder that's resting against a pole.

I hear a voice calling to me from across the street. "Do you have a radio? Can you call for help?"

I'm on South Prince Street in the city. It's known as a rough area. (Almost thirty years later, I ended up living just a few blocks down.)

From my perch on the ladder, I see a woman in a white dress across the street, pointing to the sidewalk. She doesn't say anything else—and she keeps her distance from what she's pointing to.

That can't be real! I say to myself. Leaning on my ladder, I peer through the rungs and try to focus. Shock blazes my eyes open. From twenty feet up and fifty feet away, I see a bloody mess.

Without knowing how I've done it, I'm on the ground in seconds. I rush across the busy road like a runaway train.

There sits a young black man with his back against a brick wall, bleeding. As I make it to his side, I cannot believe how much blood is oozing from his leg and pooling around his body.

He is writhing in pain. It's obvious he has crawled to this spot. The gate is open between two row houses, showing the trail he's marked by dragging his body to the sidewalk out front.

"I don't want to die!" he wails.

"What's your name?" I ask.

He rolls his head from side to side, and over and over he cries, "I don't want to die! I don't want to die!"

Then I see a geyser of blood pump from his leg. I've never had any first-aid training, but instinct kicks in. I reach in my tool belt and grab a handful of nylon tie straps. Quickly, I hook a few together and reach under his leg. The young man screams. I connect the ends of the ties above the gash in his leg and pull hard. The gush begins to slow. Now my hands are covered in his warm, sticky blood.

I look down and try to comprehend what I am seeing. His leg is broken, and the bone is protruding through his pant leg.

"What happened to you?" The words come fast.

He reaches up and grabs my shoulder, trying to pull me in close, and says in a whimpering voice, "They beat me with a baseball bat, man ..." He takes a stuttering breath. "I didn't know they'd do it, man ..." The words turn into a wail. "I don't want to die! I don't want to die!"

The sound of sirens in the city soon surrounds me. Lights flash, bodies run toward me from up and down the block.

A paramedic holding scissors and a roll of cloth squats down next to me and tears open a box of gauze. A stream of fear is soon followed by a strange, sweeping calm.

Another paramedic kneels beside me and asks me what happened.

"I don't know. I was up on that ladder when someone called me over here. The woman ... she was here ..." I look around me, but I don't see anyone but emergency personnel. "She was right here with me ..."

The first paramedic barks out a question. "Did you put these straps on?"

I'm startled, thinking I'm in trouble. "Yeah—he was bleeding really bad."

The other paramedic says quickly, "Good job, buddy! Keep holding his hand while we work on him."

I didn't realize I was holding the young man's hand. My eyes capture the sight. I see his black thumb amid his blood that is smeared on all my fingers. I had grabbed his hand to comfort him after strapping his leg, but I didn't remember doing it.

"Keep talking to him!" the first paramedic shouts. It's an order.

But I'm speechless. I don't know what to say.

The young man goes into shock, and I am pushed out of the way.

I'm sitting on the sidewalk three feet away, watching a scene from a horror movie, only it isn't dark, or raining, or in some haunted house. It's here on South Prince Street. The sun is shining, the sky is blue, but the sidewalk is puddled with blood.

I feel a tap on my shoulder. I look up and see a gun and then a badge. A policeman is standing over me. "Son, you've got a lot of blood on you," he says in a sober voice.

I notice he is wearing rubber gloves. I glance back at the paramedics. They're wearing them, too. Sitting on the sidewalk, I move my hands in front of me, palms up, and stare down at them.

Time seems to freeze. One moment in time, I am across the street up a pole, and the next, I am surrounded by yellow caution tape, ambulances, fire trucks, police cars, uniforms.

A hazmat truck pulls up. The paramedics raise the gurney and wheel the young man to the ambulance.

The police officer speaks to me again. "Do you have any open cuts or scratches on your hands?"

It strikes me like lightning.

What he is really saying is, *if this guy has AIDS, you're in trouble.*

"I don't think so. Why?"

"I'd get somewhere pretty quick and get cleaned up," he says.

Of course, it would be too late for that anyway.

He asks me a few questions and writes notes in a little notebook. I tell him about the lady who called to me from across the street and then disappeared. I tell him that I strapped the victim's leg and report what he told me about his beating.

"Probably a drug deal gone bad," he suggests, matter-of-factly. Then he tells me I can go.

I stand up, lift the yellow caution tape, and walk slowly across the street to my van. I don't have to look for oncoming traffic; the entire street is blocked by a dozen vehicles with flashing lights.

I climb into the driver's seat. Then it hits me.

I begin to weep uncontrollably. I bow my head and wipe my face on my shirtsleeve. Tears stream down my face. I sit there for a long time. I can't drive because I can't see.

In my rearview mirror, the scene is surreal. The drama—or perhaps better said, the trauma—I was a part of was so unreal. I was at the center of all of it, the first to help.

I watch as the hazmat team, wearing protective gear, begins to spray the sidewalk, washing off the lifeblood that was spilled on the concrete. The thought comes into my mind: *Everyone there was wearing some sort of protective gear, and there I was, totally unprotected.*

I never heard what happened to the young man. I never got his name.

Something else occurs to me. *Where is that woman?* I search the scene, scanning up and down the block. No white dresses. The woman who called to me has disappeared. Was she a concerned citizen who didn't want to get too involved?

Or was she an angel bringing help to a frightened young man?

Oops Again!

After a long day of installing on a Saturday, I am driving home and see the usual yard-sale sights—people milling around lawn furniture, cribs, tables with collectibles, clothing, books in boxes, and small bikes that the kids have outgrown.

I want to stop, but as I slow down enough to scan the yard, there's nothing of interest for me.

A few miles later, I see a stretch of cars along the road and a lot of people crowded under a huge tent.

This must be a killer *yard sale!* I say to myself.

I decide it's worth the stop, so I slow down and look for parking. I have to pass at least a dozen cars before I can pull over. I hop out, pat my back pocket to make sure my wallet is there, and trot back to the yard where the deals are waiting.

As I bound up the grass bank in three leaps, I notice even more cars parked all over the property. *Hmmm, maybe this is an auction.* I make my way to the tent.

People are shoulder to shoulder. I'm wondering what's on all these tables under the tent. There have to be more than a hundred people humming about.

I don't push my way through, but I do nudge between two men. One man looks over his shoulder at me and moves away.

The other, a tall man with gray hair, smiles an odd smile at me, as though we're friends. I respond with the usual "nod and pinched grin" that men do. I turn my head away from him and look down at the table.

Surprised at what I see on the table, I scowl.

The friendly man asks, "Not seeing what you're looking for?" He's referring to the different choices of food set out in aluminum trays.

I turn my attention to the kind man, my expression frozen.

"What's the matter, son? Do you need a fork or something?"

I look back at the table and survey the spread.

Then I see it. A sign hanging from the edge of the canvas tent reads, in large, black letters: "Welcome to the Statler and Finnick Family Reunion."

What do I do now?

The man slaps me on the back and says, "Well, don't be so shy. Help yourself."

I *am* hungry. I've missed lunch, and I *am* being treated like family, so I pick up a plate and start loading up.

The man walks a few feet away and grabs a few napkins and a plastic fork.

As he hands me the items, he asks, "What side of the family are you on?"

His question stops me in mid-relish-drip. I have to think quickly.

Acting surprised, I say, "You don't know?"

He cocks his head to one side. He studies my face to see if a family resemblance will help him out.

"Hmmm ... you could be from either side. Or maybe you married into the family!"

That's it. His answer gives me an idea. I don't want to lie, so I decide to be vague. I *did* marry into my wife's family, so I just answer, "You got it! I married into the family." It wasn't the Statlers or the Finnicks, but I did marry into *a* family.

He smiles and is about to walk away when I feel the strong need to 'fess up.

"Sir, I'm not part of the family. I was driving by and thought this was a yard sale." I look down at the food on my plate and back up at him. "I'll put this back."

He starts to laugh. “Oh, that’s the funniest thing I’ve ever heard!”

He turns his head to a small circle of people sitting in folding lawn chairs. “Hey, guys, this guy thought this was a yard sale!”

A few of them look up from the plates of food on their laps. Others continue their conversations. A woman from the circle of chairs calls out, “Make sure he gets some of Helen’s sun tea! It’s the best!”

I’m surprised and relieved, but I’m also embarrassed. Now I laugh, but I hold back with nervous politeness.

“Wow, thank you.” I direct my comment to the gray-haired man. “I worked all day without stopping to eat, so this is a real treat for me!”

The man grins. “No problem. Enjoy yourself. By the way, what do you do?”

My shoulders square up and I say, “I’m a cable guy, sir.”

He smiles again. “Well, cable guy, welcome to the family!”

Aron May's Story

I have often been asked if my experiences are real.

I assure you, they are.

When exchanging stories with fellow cable guys, I always appreciate a "good one!" Aron shared this one, and I asked him if I could share it with you. In his words:

This is about a customer in a retirement facility. She says, "Boy, you better hope you can fix this or I'm canceling the service."

I laugh, because it doesn't affect me.

She says, "I haven't been able to change channels all week! Watch, pushing buttons," she says. "*See?*" She looks down at the device in her hand. "You guys' service sucks!"

I crack a smile and say, "Ma'am, why are you trying to change the channels with your telephone?"

She looks down, silent for a minute. "Are you kidding me? I've watched the same stupid channel all week because of that?"

After taking the "walk of shame" in her mind, she proceeds to tell me about how she kept hearing a loud banging noise in her apartment all last night and couldn't sleep. She says she thought her roof was collapsing. I call the maintenance man right away.

The next day, he calls me back as a courtesy and tells me that they came and turned off her bathroom fan.

Thanks, Aron. Great story.

Repurposing

Everyone has a story.

I should say everyone has many stories, some of which should not be shared with a complete stranger like the cable guy.

The house was classic for harboring the stereotypical "redneck" customer. Nailed to the exterior was interior paneling printed with a stone pattern. The paneling probably didn't make it a year. It was warped, peeling, and giving up to the rain and the hot sun. Several pieces were missing.

But I can imagine that day when "Homer" hung those first few panels and then called his wife to come admire his ingenious shortcut to owning a stone house. I picture him covering her eyes from behind. When she's positioned just right, he uncovers her eyes. "Oh, Homer! It's beautiful!" Her voice has a southern twang. "Now I can tell people to look for the stone house instead of this old shack."

This all happens in a flash as I take in all of the other clues: the rusted tractor, the collection of blue fifty-five-gallon drums, the chicken coop on wheels, and the attempt to decorate using old truck tires stacked and painted bright colors.

I absolutely love this kind of customer. I could install these all day long. They are genuine, unpretentious, welcoming, hospitable, and friendly—once they know *why* you're on their property.

I've been here before. Not this exact property, but ones just like it, hundreds of times before.

I do the courteous "bump" on the horn. The short blast says

I'm here. If you slam on it or hold the horn down, well, that's just plain rude.

You announce yourself for other reasons, too. If they haven't heard you approach and you walk up on their wooden porch without warning, I guarantee there's a shotgun real close to the front door.

The other reason is simple: the dog needs to know you're coming, too.

I stay seated in my van with the window rolled down. I see Homer come out the door.

Yup, I was right. Canvas overalls with one strap hanging off his shoulder. His white T-shirt minus the sleeves is wet with sweat. He spits his tobacco out and over the wooden porch, which has no railing. He is operating within the rules of his own culture, just as I do within mine.

The installation is simple with no complications.

I install a TV in the bedroom. I turn around to see Homer sitting on the bed. Next to his side of the bed is a toilet.

"That's a great place for a toilet!" I say. "If you gotta go in the middle of the night, no need to go too far, huh?"

He looks up at me. "How much am I gonna owe ya?"

I think it's odd that he asks the question without first acknowledging my comment.

"Let's see. According to my work order, you owe sixty-five dollars."

Homer leans toward the commode and opens the lid. My eyes widen as he reaches in. He pulls out a wad of bills and counts them out, laying the money on the bed.

"Sixty-five dollars right there," he says, pointing to the small stack. He must have seen the surprised look on my face.

"This here ain't no workin' terlit," he twangs. "This bad boy was sittin' along the road, and when I seen it, I knew a good thang when I seen it. I just brought it home, cleaned it up, and *wah-lah!* I got me a cheap safe! Besides, who in their right mind is gonna look in a terlit for valuables and stuff?"

He turns toward the toilet again and opens the lid. "Ya see, I can put my pea shooter in here, my knife, my cash, and they right by my bed. If I hear a noise at night, I just flip the lid and they history!"

I'm smiling and nodding. "Interesting! And then, if a toilet breaks in the house, you already have a spare." I think I'm being helpful.

He ponders it, then runs his hand across his scraggly beard and says, "Ain't never thought of that one! I'll keep 'er in mind!"

What's Your Point?

I try really hard to be unemotional, but sometimes the irony of a situation causes me to leak sarcasm.

This customer wanted five TVs hooked up with five high-definition digital converters in her living room and four bedrooms. I really don't care how many TVs people have. I just suppose they have a reason—perhaps four teenagers, a sports-fan husband, who knows?

When I was finished connecting everything, I pulled out the channel-guide card to show her. I gestured to the long list of channels and told her she would also get forty-nine music channels.

She said, "Holy cow! Who needs all those channels? I only watch three of them." Understand: she just had *five* TVs hooked up in her house. She continued, "I mean, that's just crazy! Who needs all that?"

Seriously, lady? Who needs all that? You just had five TVs hooked up just to watch three *channels!*

I thought for a second and replied, "Do you like restaurants?"

"Of course I do."

"Do you like Chinese?" I knew she wouldn't, based on my assessment of her wall décor: black-velvet art of John Wayne and an American Indian.

"No, I hate Chinese."

I nodded. "Okay, would it be all right if your neighbor wanted Chinese?"

She seemed puzzled. "Sure, what's your point?"

I went in with my killer logic. "All these TV channels give you and everybody else a variety. It's like a city with dozens of different restaurants. You may never visit some of them, but they're available, and each restaurant serves a purpose. You may never visit the Thai, Chinese, or Indian restaurant, but many others will.

"You see, that's just like cable. There are lots of channels to serve everyone." I paused to see if any of it was sinking in. "But it doesn't mean you'll visit them just because they're in the city. You'll only dine where you're comfortable. That makes sense. Doesn't it?" I raised my eyebrows over my reading glasses, trying not to seem too facetious.

"No, I don't get what you're trying to say."

I sensed a moment of looking into the abyss and seeing no bottom. "Here's your new remote," I said.

As I handed her the remote, she looked down and said, "Is that a new remote?"

I wanted to respond, *No, it's a ham and cheese sandwich.*

Instead, I said, "Yes. It's a new remote so you can watch your three favorite channels, or," I dragged out *or,* "you can scan through, and maybe you'll find something you've never watched before on one of your five TVs."

She accepted the remote, and I turned to leave. Then, while staring at the channel-guide card, she asked, "Do all my TVs have all these channels?"

"Yes. They do."

She nodded slowly. "Great! Thank you!"

I wanted to ask her, *What's your point?* I must admit, I didn't understand. Earlier, she fussed over all the channels she *didn't* watch, but now she wanted to make sure all her TVs got everything on the list. Sometimes I wonder what's going through someone's brain. Why the change?

But I decided that it wasn't in my best interest to question her thought process. I really didn't want to know the answer anyway. I was there to do my job. I gave her more channels than she'll ever watch.

Plus a brand-new ham and cheese sandwich.

Bags o' Bugs

I was there to exchange six digital boxes.

An elderly woman sat at the kitchen table, eating a bowl of oatmeal that looked more like glue. Each time she raised her spoon to take a bite, some of the oatmeal drooped over the edge and slowly reached for the table below.

She was sitting on a wheelchair, and I noticed she had no legs. I said hello, but she just stared at me and kept eating the cold, sticky oatmeal.

As I plugged in the power cables for the new converter boxes into the electrical outlets, cockroaches poured out. I had disturbed the nest at each outlet I used. I placed the digital box on top of the TV and rotated it to access the outlet, only to see roaches scampering from their dark hiding place under the TV.

I backed up and bumped the table where the woman was sitting. She grunted, and as I turned to apologize, I noticed roaches crawling on her table as she took another bite of the sludge. With one hand, she aimed the spoon at her mouth, and with the other hand, she adeptly flicked a cockroach, which came flying toward me.

That was it. I called out for the homeowner.

"I have to go get some rubber gloves at my warehouse. I'll be back." The customer was unfazed by my remark.

I returned in thirty minutes with gloves on and plastic booties on my feet. The customer said, "Oh, you don't have to wear those booties. You can't hurt these carpets."

He didn't know I was wearing them to protect *me*! "I don't mind," was all I said.

I also brought back with me some large Ziploc bags and some roach spray. I did not dare put the old boxes I was picking up into my van the way they were.

I made no apologies as I placed an old box inside a plastic bag, liberally sprayed the contents, and zipped it up quickly. Roaches began crawling out of the box and dying inside the closed bag.

I did this six times and placed them one by one by the front door. The customer watched, almost in amusement. "Are you afraid of a few bugs?" he teased.

I snorted out my nose. "No. I'm afraid of thousands of them."

Sure, Lady, I'm from the Cable Company

I pull into a parking spot along a busy city street.

Across the street, I see an elderly lady standing at the back of her car. The trunk is open, and she is staring down at its contents.

I catch her eye as I'm getting out of my van. She calls to me. "Are you from the cable company?"

When you have appointments to install cable, often someone nearby will think you are there for them. Or they have a question about their service, and they will call out to you. Usually, they don't have an appointment set up, but they figure that while you're nearby, you would have the time to help them.

So I'm thinking she's going to ask me a cable question. "Yes, ma'am, I am."

Right away, she shouts, "Great! I have four bags of groceries I need help with."

I laugh and think to myself, *Sure! Whenever the cable company is nearby, we always help little old ladies carry their groceries in.*

I walk across the street and grab three of the bags. She picks up the last one and closes the trunk.

"Follow me," she says. We traipse through an alley, up a flight of exterior steps, and into her small kitchen. "Just put them there," she says, pointing to the counter beside the refrigerator.

Wondering if there's a cable-related question coming, I ask, "Is that all?"

"Yup. I just needed some help. Thanks, young man."

Mom's First Phone

I arrived at the house and pulled into the grassy driveway. No pavement, concrete, or gravel, just grass and mud. I stepped out carefully to avoid the mess and aimed for the thicker grass.

Before you enter a house, you'll always find clues on the outside to what it might look like on the inside. Is the mailbox marked? Are there curtains or only blinds? Is the car in the driveway inspected and in good shape, or is there dust on the dash? Do you hear a dog barking? Are there signs on the doors or windows warning trespassers of dire consequences? Do the trash cans have lids, or are the trash bags exposed? Is the siding on the house made of asbestos? If it *is* asbestos, it's a good indication that the people have lived there a long time. Otherwise, new owners would have been required to remove it or conceal it under siding.

Over the years, I have been able to prepare myself for the inside of the house by learning to read the outside.

Since asbestos was still on the outside of this house, it was a clue that the inside of the house might be in disarray.

The name on the work order was also a clue to the possible age of the owner.

I knocked on the door. A moment later, I heard a shuffling sound from inside. I knew she would be an older person by the signs I had identified and by the amount of time it took her to get to the door.

"Hello," she said in a welcoming voice.

"Hi! I'm Dan. Here to install your phone."

She was a tall, thin, elderly black woman. Her braided hair was wrapped around her head like a woven crown. She was beautiful. I found out later that she was ninety-two years old.

I finished the installation and asked her to come into the room. She lived in only two rooms of the two-story house. A cushioned chair sat in the small kitchen. The counter held a small TV.

The other room, which had probably served as her dining room in the past, was now her bedroom. The head of the hospital bed was propped up, and her nightstand was loaded with little orange medicine bottles with white caps.

The phone was plugged in and ready to use. "It's all hooked up," I said, "with your new telephone number."

She sat down very slowly, reaching for my hand to help lower her.

"I borrowed this phone from my daughter," she explained. "I don't have one, so I guess I'll have to rent one from you."

"Oh, ma'am, I don't think anyone rents phones anymore. You can buy a cheap one that works for about ten bucks." I could only imagine the story of this dear woman's life.

She looked down at the phone and asked, "How do I use it?"

I could have shown surprise, but I didn't want to embarrass her. So I said, "Well, you just pick this up and punch in the numbers of someone you want to call."

She picked up the phone and put it to her ear. I could hear the dial tone. "My daughter told me to call when you were done. But she has a cell phone, and I don't know how to call that."

She was looking up at me in an innocent way.

"Do you have her number?" I asked.

"Yes, it's right here," she said as she pulled an envelope out from under the pill bottles.

"Okay, now just touch each number as you have it written there."

She began dialing. "I know numbers but never learnt to read." She pushed the buttons and waited. "Hi, honey, it's me, Mother. Yes, he's here right now. Yes ... yes ... oh, sure, hold on."

She looked up from her spot on the edge of her bed and held the phone out to me. "My daughter wants to talk to you."

I took the phone. "Hi, this is Dan."

The voice on the other end was firm. "So she's all taken care of?"

I answered, "Yes. I guess you can see what her new number is?"

The daughter responded with a bit of her mother's story. "My mother has *never* had a phone. This isn't a *new* phone number; it's her *first* phone number. My brother lived with her but will be in the hospital for quite a while. We come by every night and eat supper with her and then put her to bed, but without my brother there, she's alone." She paused to take a breath. "My brother is seventy and lived there since Dad passed. But now he's sick and Mom lives there by herself. So thank you for getting her phone hooked up so quickly."

I nodded my head, as if she could see me, and said, "No problem. It's what I do."

I handed the phone back to "Mom," and I was surprised to see her just lay it down on the bed. "Ma'am, I think your daughter hung up, so you have to hang it up, too, or no one will be able to call you." I picked it up slowly and placed it in the cradle so she could see exactly how it was done.

"Oh ... okay," she said with a smile. "My husband and I never had a phone, and we did just fine. Nowadays, everybody has something new all the time."

Listening to her was like hearing a bird sing. The pitch of her words fluttered and waved. I smiled. "Yeah ... it's a crazy world." To which she replied, "Yes ... yes it is."

I extended my hand. She shook it and then pulled on it as a sign to help her back up. I helped her stand, then turned to the door. "Have a great day, ma'am."

I felt like she was looking through me. "Have a good day too, son."

She called me *son.*

A chill crept up my neck. Her last word was like a gift to me.

Son.

Who's the Heel? Look at His Sole

Often, I call the customers ahead of my arrival to let them know that I'll be there in a few minutes. This gives them time to put the dog out, arm themselves, or put some clothing on.

As I'm pulling into the long driveway, I notice the garage door raising. This is a good indication that they've seen me coming up the hill and they are expectantly ready to receive me.

I look over my dash to see a man in jeans, a flannel shirt, and a battered baseball cap. His sneakers are stained green from the freshly mowed yard. His down-home appearance is a welcome sight.

I hop out and make my introduction. "Hi. I'm Dan. Here to install your cable."

He raises his right hand to shake mine. "Glad you're here. We just moved in, and I'm ready for a break. I need me some TV!"

He leads me through the double-car garage, up one step and through a door that leads into an open kitchen. Beyond that is a large living room with a sixty-inch television pulled out from the wall on an angle. I always appreciate that. He knew I needed to get behind the TV, so he moved it before I arrived.

He is six or seven steps ahead of me when I notice something terribly wrong. The white plush carpet had just been installed the day before. I halt right where the kitchen linoleum stops and this fresh sea of tranquility starts.

And there they are. His sneaker prints—oil stains screaming

out the contrast between black and white. The oil's texture is still fluid, so it smears deep into the carpet's fibers with every step.

"*Whoa*!" I shout.

He turns to look back at me, shocked at my unusual tone. "What the Pete is wrong with you?" he barks.

"*Look!*" I am pointing at the tracks he's made. Just as I shout *look,* his wife walks in from the garage. I didn't know she'd pulled her car up behind my van.

I hear her keys *clank* as she tosses them on the kitchen counter and they slide a few inches. My feet are frozen in place, but my upper body turns. She immediately notices my stunned expression. She's quick to observe the mess in front of me.

Her voice is shrill. "You idiot!" she shrieks. "*I just had this installed yesterday!*"

Of course, I'm thinking she's yelling at her husband. She's not. She's looking right in my face. Her teeth clench. The husband, now turned fully to face me, says, "Yeah! Why didn't you check your shoes before you walked in here?"

I'm trapped between the two of them. My chin tucks down to my chest and my eyes slowly blink at him. "Wait a minute," I say. "Hold on *one minute.*"

I pull my leg back. I want her to see there is nothing on the bottom of my boot. I quickly lift the other one, but she's not looking at this evidence that will clear me.

She begins to rant again. "How dare you! Oh, *you* are going to pay *dearly* for this!"

I don't know whether to speak softly to disarm her or to match the tumultuous tone she is angrily throwing at me. I am also angry with the husband for blaming me so quickly.

I raise my voice. "First of all, this is as far as I have walked in *your* house. Second, I am wearing boots, and your husband is wearing sneakers." I am shouting, at this point. "If you would just stop yelling and *look* at his shoes and then look at the bottom of mine, you will see that *I,*" I say *I* very firmly "am not tracking oil in your house!"

She breathes. He looks down at his feet. I look at him and then back at her, then back at him again. The anticipation is agonizing.

Finally, he begins to walk back in my direction, and there they are: more fresh tracks of oil.

"You idiot!" she shrieks again. "*Take off your shoes!*" He stops in mid-stride and leans down to pull off one of his sneakers.

She loses it again. She comes around me and begins to berate him unmercifully in front of me.

Now I'm thinking, *Is this a good time to ask where they want the other TVs hooked up?*

I keep my mouth shut. He realizes he is the culprit. Even though I am innocent of tracking oil in the house, she is very curt with me until the installation is over.

Nowadays, I wear booties on my feet before entering a house, but I will never forget that one. And now, when someone wants me to enter through the garage, I check my shoes.

I check theirs, too.

Sometimes a Little Thing Is a Big Thing

My work order states: "audio works but no picture." This is a first. (Not that I haven't seen odd things, right?)

I knock on the door.

A woman in her late sixties answers and says immediately, "I should have canceled, but I wanted to make sure it wasn't your cable box."

It's a legitimate statement. It happens that digital boxes, with their many components, could have an issue.

"Here it is." She points to her living room TV. "My VCR works fine, but I can't watch cable on it."

I get behind the set and look at the connections. Everything looks correct. I change the input on the TV to A/V, for audio/video input, and start a videotape. It plays a tape from a show she recorded ten years ago.

I change the input to channel 3. Nothing. The screen goes blank. I check the connections again. They are correct.

"Hmmm ..." I scratch my head like I am deep in thought. "When did it stop working?"

"The tuner is shot. It hasn't worked for years. I just use this TV to watch my tapes."

I must look perplexed, with my eyebrows bunched up.

She says, "I have three TVs, so I went to the cable company and picked up three of these digital boxes and hooked them up myself."

I nod. "Well, you did a good job, but this TV here," I point with authority, "is broken. The tuner isn't working, so you have a few choices. You can bring one of your other TVs out here, buy a new TV, or just use this TV for watching tapes."

She begins to grimace. "I don't want to buy another TV. I just hate to get rid of it. I bought it at a yard sale twenty-four years ago, and it's worked fine for all those years."

"Are you saying it's worked fine for watching tapes or watching cable?"

She quickly responds, "Oh, it's never worked for TV channels, only for watching tapes."

I try to be crystal clear. "But if you want to watch cable on it, channel 3 has to work. Otherwise, it is simply a monitor for the VCR."

She crosses her arms. "I thought maybe you could fix it."

"Sorry, ma'am, we don't fix TVs." I pause for her acknowledgment. "Tell you what. I can put your VCR tuner on channel 3 and see if that works."

Immediately, she yells, "No, no, don't do that! I won't know how to get it back!"

I am startled. I'm trying to help her use the TV for both purposes, but she is adamant and begins to decline all my suggestions.

I decide to speak slowly. "Okay, ma'am, if I understand you correctly, the reason I am here today was to make this work, and now that I figured out a way to make it work, you don't want me to?"

Her lips flatten as she closes her mouth tightly. She grimaces as though she is in pain. She reminds me of a TV game show contestant whose face contorts over the agony of having chosen the wrong answer.

She begins to clench her fists and pump them up and down as though she's beating on a drum. My eyes widen. I'm waiting for a volcanic eruption.

She stares intently at the TV while her pumping fists beat the air. Her squinting eyes open suddenly.

I feel my feet starting to slide backward in case she attacks.

Then she breaks. Her hands fly to her sides like the wings of a bird. Her mouth opens wide as she shouts, "Just leave me alone!"

Now I am backing up. "Ma'am?"

"Just leave. You should have never come here."

I'm already moving sideways toward the door, and I'm keeping my eyes on her. My hand reaches for the door handle. "Okay, ma'am, I'm leaving. Okay? Is that all right?"

She turns her attention from the TV and looks me in the eye. "Sorry, it's just too much for me, too much. I need this for my tapes!" Her voice cracks with emotion.

"No problem. I hope you have a good day!"

I close the door behind me and scurry down the steps, trying to get to my van as quickly as possible.

I hear the house door open. Out of the corner of my eye, I see the woman coming out. I round the front of my van and open the door, scuffing skin off the top of my head as I scramble in. My windows are cracked, so I can easily hear her voice again. "Sir? Sir?"

I'm not sure if I should get out or drive off. I pretend I don't hear her. She calls again, "Sir! Sir?"

I grunt and turn my head back toward the house, rolling down my window to be courteous. "Yes?"

"Did I need to sign something?"

"Nope, we know where you live!" I shout with a smile and drive off.

In this job, you never know what you'll be walking into—or trying to get out of!

Put Some Clothes On!

You would think people would wear appropriate clothing when they answer the door.

It has happened enough that now that it doesn't surprise me. But years ago, it came as a great shock and made me feel very uncomfortable.

A graduate student at Franklin & Marshall College opens the door of her studio apartment wearing nothing but a bath towel and a small towel on her head. Her shoulders are still wet with droplets of water. She has just gotten out of the shower.

"C'mon in," she says.

"Oh, excuse me," I reply in a hugely apologetic tone.

"Don't worry about it. The TV is over there."

She points to a nightstand at the foot of her bed, with a large TV perched precariously on top. I look for the cable wire coming in from the outside, just below the window.

I purposely avert my eyes as I turn to go out her door. "I'll go outside to turn the cable on," I tell her. "I'll be at least fifteen minutes, so that will give you some time." I assume she knows what I mean: *I will be gone for fifteen minutes, so you can get dressed!*

I climb in my van and immediately call dispatch. "I'm at a customer's house and she answered the door with no clothing on but a towel." Documenting my time is important. At least it is to me. I want the company to *know* when I arrived and when I'll be leaving. The time it will take to hook up the cable at the pole and at the TV will be no more than twenty minutes.

I knock on the door again.

"C'mon in," she says a second time.

I walk in to the see the *same sight*, only this time, she is sitting on the edge of her bed, doing her nails. Fifteen minutes! Seriously, you can't get dressed in fifteen minutes?

Carefully averting my eyes again, I stare at the TV and connect the wire, then ask her to sign the work order.

She leans forward, holds the towel in place, and writes her name.

I tear off the carbon and say, "Here's your copy."

She looks up at me, almost daring me to stare at her.

I don't. I look down at my clipboard and leave.

Here's another one.

The appointment is in the time frame of 8:00 a.m. to noon. The house is not even two minutes from the office. So you might think that this girl would assume, *They're so close, I'm sure I'll be the first one*. Uh-uh. She thinks, *I know ... I'll go take a shower!*

I knock on the door. She opens the door with just a towel wrapped around her. She's brushing her teeth.

"Oh, excuse me ... here to hook up your Internet."

She turns and points up the steps. "It's up here." She walks ahead of me up the stairs.

I guess since I'm old enough to be her father, she isn't feeling threatened in the least.

Here's one more.

I go up to a second-floor apartment and introduce myself.

The female customer shows me where everything is to be installed.

"I'll be back. Need to get your equipment and get you hooked up at the pole."

Minutes later, I re-enter the apartment, only to hear water running. *She's in the shower!*

Who gets in the shower when a strange man is in their apartment?

I leave immediately and head downstairs to a law office that's directly below her apartment. "Hi, I'm from the cable company. I am installing at the apartment upstairs. I left her apartment for a few minutes to hook her up at the pole, and when I went back in, she was in the shower."

The receptionist bolts back in her chair and accusingly asks, "How do *you* know she's in the shower?"

I smirk. "Do you hear the water in the pipes behind you? Well, that's the shower. That's how I know."

I sit down in the office waiting room and wait at least twenty minutes until neither of us can hear the shower running.

Okay, last one. Really.

I knock. An eighteen-year-old woman answers the door in her underwear and bra.

I am shocked. I really am. I introduce myself. "Cable man." I quickly follow up with, "Is this your parents' house?"

She responds through the screen door, "Yes. You're here to turn on the cable, right?"

"Yes, but I have to ask if you are eighteen years or older, and could you put some clothes on?"

Sarcastically, she says, "*Yes, I am* eighteen, and dude, I wear less than this at the beach!"

Well, perhaps her bikini *does* have less material than her underwear, but seriously—*put some clothes on!*

Friend in a Box

Often, installing cable requires moving *something.*

It's amazing to me. They know you're coming. They made the appointment, but the room you're to work in is buried with stuff.

I walk into a trailer. The TV is in front of a window. The curtains are heavy, and dust clings to them like moss to a tree.

"Sir, would you mind if I pull these curtains back so I can see what I'm doing behind your TV?"

He clears his throat and a piece of food shoots across the room toward me. "Go ahead. Do you need my help moving the TV?"

"No, I got it," I say as I drag this 1980 floor-model TV across the dingy carpet. The growth of dirt static-clinging to the back consists of cat hair, dust, spiderwebs, and shreds of cloth that mice have left behind.

My boot hits a box tucked close beside the TV. I look down. It's a solid wooden box with a unique design. The box appears to be mahogany, with an inlaid copper thread running around all four edges of the lid. A metal clasp secures the contents. It looks expensive and seems out of place in this home. I don't want to damage it.

Before I bend over to slide it out of the way, I brush the layer of dust off the top. I am surprised to see a shiny, two-inch-by-five-inch nameplate square in the middle. I look back at the customer. For a second, he isn't looking. I look down again and use my bare hand to brush off the remaining dust, revealing a name. Not just a name, but two dates as well.

"Sir, would you move this box?"

He looks up from his magazine. "Ohhhh ... you found Richard."

He pushes himself up from the well-worn, padded armchair and brushes the cheese-curl crumbs from his "wife beater" T-shirt. "That's Richard. He's my buddy."

I stand straight up and back away to make room.

"Yeah, we've been friends all our lives. He died, and his family wouldn't take him."

A bit morbid, I'm thinking. The date shows that his friend died more than twenty-five years ago, and here his cremated remains sit beside a TV, forgotten by family and covered in dust.

I say, "A little Pledge would really make that shine," trying to prompt a bit more care for the remains in the box.

"I used to have him on top of the TV," he says, "but those darn cats kept knocking him on the floor."

Later, I come home and tell my wife, "If I am cremated, do *not* give my box to anyone. Put me in the ground!"

First on the Accident Scene

I hadn't driven around this bend for quite some time.

I had been working on the east side of the river, but on this day, I ran an installation route on the west side.

I was driving north on Norrisville Road, leaving Jarrettsville, Maryland, traveling around fifty miles an hour. As is common with me, I glanced to my right and left and noticed the houses I've been in. As amazing as it may sound after doing more than thirty thousand installations, I can remember the inside of the house and sometimes the personalities, the pets, and where I put the wires.

I drove cautiously around the bend, braking carefully, when suddenly, I had a flashback. It was like it was yesterday:

Ahead of me is a sight my mind cannot comprehend, not at first.

A car is upside down, the tires spinning freely.

I slam on my brakes and pull over as far as I can. As I jump out of my van, I twist my ankle. I hear a crack, but I keep running.

The car's engine is racing; its horn is blaring.

Chills run up my spine. Lying on the upturned ceiling is a detached head. It's turned away from me.

Time slows, and the horn begins to drone. I stop cold; my boots scuff the gravel and spray it like buckshot against the metal doors of the car.

"Help me." I hear the voice coming from the other side of the car.

There she is, her face covered in dirt from the road. Her hands, arms, and legs are bloody from the broken glass. The roof had collapsed, and the window was her only escape. She's had to slide her head sideways to get through the nine-inch gap.

I help her up, but only to her knees. She falls against me.

I shout, "We have to get away from the car!" Fearing a gas leak or another speeding vehicle heading our way, she gets up, and we move thirty feet away.

A car comes by. The driver looks over but keeps going. Then Steve Ceraso, my company supervisor, just happens to be driving by. He stops and runs over to us.

As Steve kneels down beside the injured woman, I tell him, "I have some water in my van. I'll be right back."

I run for my van, but I fall. My ankle. Pain sears, and then it leaves. I retrieve two bottles and give her one to drink. She is shaking from shock. Steve calls 911.

I open the other bottle, douse a few paper towels, and wipe the dirt from above her eyes. "Thank you, thank you, " she keeps repeating as she weeps and sips the water as she's rocking on the side of the road.

Suddenly, I remember the other head I had seen.

"Were you alone?"

She nods as she swallows the cold water. "Yes ... yes ... I was going too fast ..." She is trying to catch her breath.

I look over at the car, where I see the hair. "There's a head in your backseat."

She says, "I'm in cosmetology school. That's a dummy head."

Deep sigh! "Dang, girl! I thought it was *real!*" She laughs.

A few weeks later, I got a letter in the mail with a picture of a pretty young lady. It was a letter from her father. I read it to my wife. I only remember one sentence: "Here's a picture of my daughter without dirt on her face." I laughed. I would never have recognized her.

"Wow, she's pretty," said my wife.

I replied, “All I saw was a dirty, scuffed-up face and a bloodied body.”

I never wrote back. I have since lost the letter and the picture, but whenever I drive around that corner, I see the ghost image of that car, and I thank God that he was watching out for her.

The Bill Was $15.95, but I Left with $120

"All I have is a hundred-dollar bill. Do you have change?"

When collecting the COD (cash on demand) for services, I often collect a check or money order for the cable company. This person wants to pay cash. The bill is less than twenty dollars, and he asks if I have change for a hundred-dollar bill.

"No, I don't have change, but I can give you a receipt that you paid a hundred dollars, and you'll have a few months' credit."

I watch as the customer's head jerks back in utter shock. "What? I'm not paying for a few months in advance!"

I nod. "Okay. Let me ask you a question. Are you planning on living here for the next two months?"

He scowls. "Of course. I just moved in here. I'm not leaving for at least a year." I am hoping he follows my reasoning.

"Good. Because I don't have change, and if you're planning on keeping the basic cable service anyway, you'll be ahead of the game. No cable bill for a few months, and less to worry about while you get settled in. Sounds fair, doesn't it?"

He pauses and then says, "You know what, that makes sense."

He hands over the hundred-dollar bill, reaches into his pocket, and then hands me a twenty-dollar bill.

"What's this for?" I ask him.

He responds, "You did such a good job, and I always believe in tipping someone who does a good job."

I'm flabbergasted. His connection fee was $15.95. He could have used the twenty for that.

Mr. & Mrs. Parker

The cheerful man met me at the door.

"Here to install my cable, right?" The knot of his tie peeked out over the top of his buttoned-up cardigan.

I nodded.

"Come in. I'll show you where we want them."

We is always a key word. It means there is someone else in the house who has some sort of decision-making authority.

"My name is Mr. Parker, and over there at the dining room table is Mrs. Parker."

Mrs. Parker looked up from her coffee and the newspaper open flat on the table. She made no effort to hide the fact that she wore a nightgown and bunny slippers and had curlers in her hair. She was smiling and chewing at the same time, and she glanced at me and then returned to her paper.

Mr. Parker whistled as we walked down a narrow hallway. I followed him into a bedroom painted in shades of green. There was a single bed, a dresser, and a nightstand with a lamp that showered light on a stack of books. Economics, history, and philosophy books stood in a neat pile, with the bindings aligned perfectly. On the dresser was a black and white TV. *Maybe it's a guest room set up for a visitor*, I guessed.

I guessed wrong.

"This is my room, and I want that TV hooked up," Mr. Parker said as he pointed to the set that was situated in the middle of the dresser. The TV sat in the center, as if there were no other purpose for the top of the dresser. Nothing else shared the space—no coins, papers, or keys.

Mr. Parker spoke again. "And if you will follow me, I will show you Mrs. Parker's room." We left his bedroom and went to the next room. The room was yellow with frilly curtains, another single bed, and a nightstand with an alarm clock, a few magazines, and a hairbrush.

He pointed to the television sitting on a rectangular coffee table with a cloth runner beneath the TV.

"And this one," he said.

"Okay, Mr. Parker, I'll get my tools and cable. I'll be drilling through the floor into the basement. Where is the basement?"

He paused. "Oh yes, the basement. That's out in the kitchen. Let me see if Mrs. Parker is decent." I thought this was odd since he had already introduced us from afar, but I didn't question his thought process.

We walked down the hallway, Mr. Parker leading the way. As we rounded the corner into the kitchen, Mrs. Parker was biting into a piece of toast. As a courtesy, I stopped a few feet behind Mr. Parker.

"Mrs. Parker, this is the cable man. Are you decent enough to show this man the basement?"

She chewed for a second or two. "Can't you, Mr. Parker?" She sounded frustrated.

"But Mrs. Parker, my knees don't like the stairs," he said quickly, then turned back to me with a sheepish, embarrassed look. The couple calling each other *Mr.* and *Mrs.* was a bit unnerving. I didn't get a sense that they were married but rather were practicing a formal living arrangement.

I interrupted the standoff. "Mr. Parker, I can find the basement. I do this all the time."

He looked at her. "Is that okay, Mrs. Parker?" She nodded as she bit into the toast again.

I walked past her and down a flight of steps to figure out where the wires would be coming down. When I came back upstairs, I moved some of the furniture in either room to make space for me to work. I drilled the holes, pushed the wires down, and then found them in the basement where I thought they would be.

Entering Mr. Parker's bedroom, I saw him measuring the floor from wall to wall. Then he measured the dresser width, and on a piece of paper, he began making notes.

"Is everything okay?" I asked.

He was uncomfortable. "Umm, yes. It's just that ... when you moved my dresser and put it back, it's not in the center of the room anymore."

I stepped back and looked at either side of the dresser. It looked the same to me.

He pulled out his measuring tape. "You see, here on the left side, from the dresser to the wall, it's fifty-one and one-half inches, but on the right side ..." He moved to the right side of the dresser with his tape, pulled it out, and said, "It's fifty-three inches."

My mouth dropped open an inch. I was hoping he wouldn't measure it.

He was agitated. "I had it centered, and when you moved the TV on the top of the dresser to screw in the cable, now *it's* not centered anymore, either."

He started measuring again. "I can't move this dresser myself, so you'd better help me before you leave. I can't sleep if it's not right."

My mouth was still gaping. I responded, "Sure, sir."

He turned and looked right in my eyes. "My name is Mr. Parker."

My mouth kept going into gape mode. I couldn't help it. "I am sorry, *Mister Parker.* I will help you."

We gently slid the dresser to the right. He measured. "Nope! That's too far." Back a half inch. Measured again. "Almost!" I slid it ever so slightly; the dresser didn't even seem to be moving. Suddenly he shouted, "*Stop!* That's it. That's where it belongs."

To make sure, he measured both sides, from the furniture to each wall. "Perfect. Now, let's do the TV."

Mouth gaping again, I said, "You want the TV in the exact center, too?"

He looked at me, surprised. "That's how it was before you got here. That's how it will be when you leave."

After several attempts, the TV was perfectly centered, and he clipped the measuring tape onto his belt. "There." He smiled, back to his cheerful self. "I feel better. Now, let's make sure Mrs. Parker's room is back to normal."

By this time, Mrs. Parker had walked by his room and was in her room.

We entered. "Mrs. Parker," he announced as he pulled the tape from his belt, "I want to tidy this up."

"Mr. Parker, you know you are not allowed in this room when I am in here."

He stopped in his tracks. "Well, Mrs. Parker, I can tidy this up later, when you take a shower." He was looking down at the cloth runner under the TV. It wasn't perfectly flat and balanced on either side of the table. He looked bothered at the sight and was visibly shaking.

She spoke. "Mr. Parker. Leave it alone!"

Her words were firm, and his cheerful smile turned upside down. "Yes, Mrs. Parker."

We both backed out of the room.

Sometimes, you just don't ask.

You Can't Watch TV on a Deserted Island

So, if I lose power, can I still watch the cable? You know, like when the power goes out, you can still use the telephone."

Did the customer really ask me that?

I respond with a question of my own. "Let me ask you a question. If you are shipwrecked on a deserted island, who needs to be rescued?"

He looks at me and answers, "I do."

"Right!" He is staring at me, much like you would be if you were there.

Then I ask, "Do you have a generator?"

"No. Why would I need a generator?"

"Does your TV have batteries?"

"No."

I go for the kill. "Then if the power goes out and the cable is still on, how are you going to turn on your TV?"

He ponders my wisdom. "Oh, I get it. No electricity, no TV."

I wink and do the *tsk* sound. "You got it!"

He smiles, and then his eyebrows make a tight formation. "Wait! What's that got to do with me on an island?"

"I don't know," I say, "I just threw it out there."

I was in an ornery mood that day.

The Customer Really Said That

The cable lines have just been run down the street, and the salespeople have made their rounds to sign people up. Appointments are made, and now it's my turn to make it happen.

I knock on the door to do a new installation.

A lady pulls back the curtain and peeps out the window beside the front door. I smile, nod, and say loudly enough for her to hear me through the double-pane window, "I'm here to install the cable."

She responds, "Do you have to come inside?"

Did the customer really say that?

Puzzled, I say, "Do you watch your TV outside?"

She says, "No, we watch it in the living room."

"Well, then, yes. I do need to come inside."

I enter a house to hook up a PC to the Internet. The daughter is playing a game or something. The mother says, "You are so lazy! Get off that computer and go watch some TV!"

Did the customer really say that?

Running a new cable line to a customer's house requires what's called a mid-span connection. Where the house is situated, all the utilities run to a pole directly in front of the house. If you connect to the house and run straight to the pole, the cable line will rub through the shingles.

So you run the house connection to the wire that goes from

pole to pole. This is called the strand wire. It's what supports the cable. You place your ladder hooks over this strand wire. As the wire sways forward and backward and most definitely sags, you make a connection there.

While I'm making this connection to the strand wire, my ladder is leaning toward the house. I am in the wind, focusing on getting this dangerous portion of the installation done.

Suddenly, I hear the customer's voice. "You better not fall. You would die!"

Did the customer really say that?

So I holler back, "If I fall, could you please call my wife and my children and tell them that the last words I heard were yours!"

Sir, You Really Don't Want to Do That!

I was greeted at the door by a customer carrying a measuring tape. He announced, "I've already measured where I want you to drill the hole."

No "Hello," not "How you doing?" Just right to the point.

"Okay, well, let's see what you got."

Instead of walking to the living room where the TV would be, he led me directly to the basement.

"Okay, now, do you see that black magic marker up there on the plywood?"

I looked up at the ceiling to see the black *X* that marked the spot.

"Yes, I see it. Can we go upstairs to see where we're drilling down through the floor?" I said this to take control of the situation.

"No, we're not drilling down; we're drilling up!" he said with a certainty in his voice.

"Hmmm," I murmured. "May I see the TV upstairs first?"

He looked at me impatiently. "Sure, but I measured everything before you got here to make it easy on you."

I nodded and replied, "Of course, I understand. But show me where the wire will come through."

We went upstairs to the carpeted living room, which was in immaculate shape, with matching couches and drapes. A potted plant sat on the coffee table. Everything was in perfect order, except that the TV was pulled a few feet from the wall.

As I headed out to my van, I said, "I'll go get my drill and some cable."

When I knew I was out of his earshot, I said out loud to myself, "Here we go!"

I returned to the living room with my equipment, and the customer said, "Let's go downstairs where I have everything marked."

He was so proud of himself, but I was certain he didn't understand the way an installation is done. I obliged him and walked with him down to the basement.

"Here." He looked up at the ceiling, at his brilliant marking. "Drill here."

Was he serious? He wanted me to drill *up?*

"Sir, I am not going to drill up into your living room. I drill down."

He didn't like my tone. "Now listen to me, young man," he said, "I know my measurements are accurate, and I know if you drill here, you will come up exactly where I want the cable to be."

Didn't he make the appointment for the cable company to come out and install the cable? Why didn't he drill this hole before I got there?

"Sir, I am not going to drill up. If I drill down, the wood will splinter down instead of up, and no damage will be done to your carpet. I guarantee it."

He was frustrated with me now; I could see it in his face. So I offered him my drill.

"If you want to drill this hole," I said, "here's my drill." I handed it to him and he grunted and said, "Fine!"

As a precaution, I said, "Before you drill this hole, I need to write on my work order that you wanted to drill the hole. I just need you to sign this right here." He signed the form.

Then he plugged in the drill, stood on the small stepladder, and squeezed the trigger. Of course, the drill sped easily though the plywood, and then it broke through. He kept pushing as the drill spun through the carpet padding and the carpet above.

Then the drill yanked to one side and almost threw him off the stepladder.

He reversed the spin and then switched to forward again. Back and forth, he commanded the electric tool to do its duty for him. Finally, the drill bit extended the entire way through the basement ceiling, and then he reversed it to bring it out.

It was stuck.

He pulled on it with the power off. The drill wouldn't budge. He reversed the bit, and reluctantly it came down, bringing small, white puffs of material with it. I knew what had happened but had no idea how bad it would be.

Drilling down through carpet allows you to feel the surfaces you are going through. The drill becomes an extension of your senses. Often, you pull a section of carpet away from the wall or cut a small slice in it, so as not to catch the fibers.

First, you feel the carpet fibers separate as you slowly turn the bit. The underlayment is next. Once you're through that 1/4-inch layer, you hit plywood, typically 5/8-inch, which gives you the feel of solid structure, and you can increase the speed of the drill to get through.

Drilling *up* is a huge mistake. The false security provided by the plywood allows you to drill fast with no time to slow down when entering the next layer, which is the underlayment. The padding is like a blanket and needs a gentle turn, but from below, there's no telling when you're through to that level. Next, you reach the carpet, which is like a weave. Catch it wrong and it will bind or tear, or the drill bit will puncture the carpet like a bullet through a pumpkin.

We walked upstairs. I couldn't bear to see what he did. In a way, I wanted him to mess it up. He didn't trust me to do my job the way I was trained, so all bets were off. He would have to take full responsibility for this one.

Sure enough, as we rounded the corner, his jaw dropped, and mine, well ... I hid my smile. The drill had caught the padding and it wrapped around the bit, which pulled it from its staples. The result was a mound about six inches high and a hole in the carpet that looked like a shotgun had blown through it from below. The padding bunched up, and the carpet was shredded in a three-inch diameter cavity. It almost looked like a small volcano had erupted against his perfect living room wall.

"Oh, crap!" he cried. "My wife is going to kill me!"

I tried to keep the smile hidden. "I told you in the basement that you never drill up through carpet."

He didn't hear me. He raced over to the wall and started jumping up and down on the protrusion.

"Sir," I said, "the padding is now missing in this horseshoe shape. You're going to have to remove the carpet, re-pad the floor, and replace the carpet to make it right. I am sorry, but I tried to warn you."

Now he looked scared. Earlier, he was a man of supreme confidence because he had measured and found the perfect sweet spot. He failed to consider that he had hired a professional. He decided he could do it better.

A Strange Request

I was there to program two remotes for two TVs that were within five feet of each other. The one remote kept changing channels on both TVs, and the customer, an older man in his seventies, wanted to be able to watch two shows at the same time.

The process was simple. Install an infrared eye to the left of one TV and an infrared eye on the right side of the other TV. Once done, both remotes worked. The volume worked independently, and so did the channels.

He chattered nonstop about his wife thinking he was crazy for having two TVs side by side. I didn't want to tell him, but it *was* somewhat odd.

I remember many years ago installing two TVs in a living room for two deaf brothers. One couch faced one wall and the other couch faced another. That way, the brothers could be in the same room and still watch different TV channels.

In this case, the man wanted both a game show and the news playing simultaneously. The chatter from both was disorienting to me.

"Janet, you can choose the prize in the middle ... of China, where nuclear submarines were launched in a show of strength ... Janet, you can choose to keep ... both submarines, which have the capability of striking ... your new dishwasher!"

The deafening volume was giving me a headache, but the man, who had two hearing aids, was in tune with both broadcasts.

"How can you differentiate the two shows, sir?" I asked, with all sincerity.

"Oh, my one hearing aid is off." This was a simple answer, but I couldn't help thinking that *both* TV shows made it to either ear!

Then we were finished.

The question he was about to ask was so bizarre, I asked him to repeat it. "What did you ask?"

The man, who was wearing pajamas, stood up from his chair. "I've had my dog locked up since you came. I'm going to let him out to see if he'll bite you. Is that all right?"

He wanted to see if his dog will bite me. I had never heard that one. *Hold still; don't move. I want to see if my dog will bite you.* It was a strange request.

I said, "Well, I would prefer *not* to be bitten today. Maybe tomorrow!"

He didn't hear me. I must have been on the side with the hearing aid turned off.

I sat on the couch and braced myself as he brought out a small, black dog with gray whiskers. He held the dog and leaned down toward me. "There, there, Mutton," he said to the small pet. "See, he's not a bad man." The man held the dog closer to me.

"Go ahead, try to pet him," the man said.

I spoke softly. "Hey, buddy. How are you?" Fully expecting a nip, I kept my hand closed with no fingers extended. The dog winced but bent his head as my fist rubbed against his ear.

"See, Mutton, he's a nice man," the old man said, calmly reassuring his dog. Now I'm thinking, *Hey mister, how about reassuring me!*

Mutton let me pet him and didn't bite, but as I left, I wondered, *What kind of person asks such a strange question: "May I see if my dog will bite you?"*

Then I answered myself. *Someone with two TVs in his living room.*

Jeff Barker and the Cat

For a contractor, job security is based on quality of work and customer satisfaction. However, the budget of the corporation can always override the contractor's best work ethics and solid reputation.

As it was, I was working for a small cable company that was being bought out by a larger company. When the merger happened, I began to meet all the employees of the new company as they walked in wearing red shirts with the company logo prominently displayed.

"Hi, I'm Dan Armstrong. What's your name?" I would say each day to the new faces I was meeting.

One day, a young man walked in the back door. I hadn't met him yet, so as he shuffled by, I asked him for his name. He was wearing a hooded sweatshirt, his hands buried in the pockets.

"Hi, I'm Dan Armstrong. What's your name?"

He stopped abruptly, lowered his head, and glared at me. "Jeff Barker."

So for weeks, whenever he would stroll by, I would say, "Hey, Jeff!" To which he would nod and keep walking with a smirk on his face. He wasn't friendly at first, but eventually, he did warm up to me.

One day, he was staring at his phone and I said, "Hey, Jeff." He didn't respond. *Maybe he didn't hear me.* So I said it a little louder. "Hey, Jeff—Jeff Barker!"

He kept staring down. Another installer at the table asked, "Why are you calling him Jeff Barker? That's not his name."

I looked at the installer then at "Jeff" and asked, "Hey, man, what's your real name?" He looked up from his phone and slowly said, "Michael Friend."

I cocked my head and with a suspicious smile asked, "Now, is that your *real* name?" His face broke into a smile and he responded, "Yes, that *is* my real name."

I didn't ask him until years later, why the ruse? He said he was just playing with me because I wasn't a company man; I was a contractor.

A short time later, he happened upon me at a job while I was installing an outside cable line. The weather had turned, and I'd forgotten to bring my winter coat. I was shivering.

I came down from the ladder and he said, "Dude, you look cold."

I nodded. "Yeah, I forgot my coat." He promptly reached into his van and pulled out a coat with the company logo on it. He was getting a new one in a few days, but it was a very kind gesture for him to give me his winter coat.

We bump into each other quite often, and we rarely call each other by our real names.

"Hey, Nelson!" I will call out. He returns, "Hi, Gary!"

We met at a convenience store the other day. We were both coming out of the store with fresh coffees, trying to warm ourselves from the cold day.

"Hey, Jeff Barker, got any cable stories?" I asked with a laugh.

"Actually, I do. Have I ever told you the 'dead cat' story?"

I was intrigued. Mornings at the cable company will often find the guys exchanging stories of their previous day's events with much emotion, expression, and surprise. But we were alone, and I had to hear this one without interruption.

In Michael's words, here's what happened:

"I knocked on a door. A real old lady answered after quite

awhile. I was there to pick up a box that she wasn't using anymore. It was, like, ninety degrees outside, and as soon as I walked in, I smelled the stench of death. It was, like, 105 degrees in the house, and the smell was revolting." Michael paused and grimaced at his recollection. "I step in the door, and it stinks really bad. I look down at the floor and there's this cat. It's real still and it doesn't move.

"So I ask the lady if that cat will move, because I don't want to step on it. And the lady tells me that the cat is asleep. Well, I'm looking down at this cat and I'm looking at her and I'm thinking that she has got to be crazy or senile.

"I put my boot against the cat and nudge it. The lady says, 'Don't do that, you'll wake him up, honey.' She's trying to be nice to me and be firm at the same time. So I say to her, 'Ma'am, I think your cat is dead!'"

Michael now started to laugh, and I grunted with laughter.

"So I put my boot on the cat again, and this time I nudge it a bit harder and it slides on the linoleum floor. I say, 'Ma'am, your cat is dead!'

"She just looks at me from her chair and says, 'No, no, he's asleep.'

So I say to her, 'Why don't you pick it up?'

She gets up and walks over real slow, because she's, like, ninety years old, and she bends over and picks up this dead cat. I am backing up because it smells so bad! The legs are all stiff. And she starts talking to it.

Man, I went to pick up her box at her TV and the cat hair was so thick, it was like a glove! I was leaving as she was putting the cat down, and she said that she was upstairs for the last five days and must have forgotten to feed the cat. Not to mention, Dan, it was over a hundred degrees in there. I'm telling you, that cat was cooked!"

Why do I tell this story? I want you to know that I'm not the only cable guy who has these adventures. Just ask any cable man, and you'll find out we don't need to watch TV.

Our jobs provide us with enough entertainment.

What *Is* That Up There?

The customer shows me his master bedroom, where he wants a cable outlet. The best way to get the cable where he wants it is for me to drop a wire down from the attic.

I always look around the room, just in case they may have missed the outlet on the wall, or perhaps another outlet in the room leads to the attic and I can split off of it.

As I'm looking around, I notice that the drywall ceiling above their queen-size bed is discolored and bulging.

I point to the anomaly. "What's that?"

"We don't know. We just started noticing it a few weeks ago, and I haven't had the time to call someone to check it out. There's no water coming through, and it hasn't rained for weeks, so it's a mystery."

I move closer to the edge of the bed. "Well, I have to go up in your attic, so I'll peek over there." I pause and glance up at the shape on the ceiling. *That's just strange.*

The customer shows me the access panel in the closet. I get my tools and ladder and make the ascent into the dangerous unknown.

Slowly, I move the access panel to the left. Then I hear something. It's a noise I've heard before, but it's out of place. *What is that noise?*

I pull myself up, careful not to hit my head on the nails that hold the shingles in place. I've scratched my head dozens of times, despite my cautious movements.

The flashlight in my mouth only casts a small beam of light. I am accustomed to seeing the light create shadows from dust particles as I crawl on top of undisturbed insulation. But the shadows I'm seeing are much larger. They appear to be bugs floating in the air.

The noise is soon to become more familiar and the danger more evident.

The customer hollers up from his closet, "What do you see?" I really don't have time to solve his mystery. I just want to minimize my time in the fiberglass-polluted air. Drill my hole, drop a wire, and get out of there.

But I am curious about what is directly above his bed. What is happening to the drywall? I do my work and make my way to the open access panel.

"Sir, I'm going to hand you my drill, and then I'll crawl over and see what I can find out for you."

He accepts the drill and places it on the floor. I turn toward the area where the bed below is situated. I am thinking, *I have to crawl sixteen feet, pull the insulation up and look around, breathe in this stuff*—I had forgotten my mask—*and crawl back. Sure hope this guy appreciates this extra effort.*

I begin the careful crawl. Just so you understand the way houses are built: the attic has no floor. The ceiling joists are two feet apart, with insulation filling the gaps.

The surface that my knee is on is at most two inches wide. Every two feet, I have to find the two-inch target with my hands and then my knees. It's a delicate crawl that reminds me of a cheetah whose concentration is synchronized with his body. Eyes on the gazelle, he lifts one leg slowly, and the other follows. If I put my knee on anything other than a two-inch stud, I will fall through the ceiling.

The shadows from the small flashlight's beam become more numerous. As I move closer to my target, I stop. Something is crawling on my neck. Balancing with one knee on a stud and the other knee two feet behind me, I lift my right hand and slap my neck.

"Ouch!" I look up in a diagonal direction above the area where the mystery stains are located. "*What is that?*" I say out loud. It's an organic-looking, upside-down triangle, brown with many crevices in it. I move two feet closer.

Then the shadows are no longer ephemeral. They are real. The humming noise is more real. And the recent stinging sensation on my neck and the sight I've just seen are causing me great concern.

With the flashlight in my mouth, I look down, and there it is. The cause of the ceiling stain is now obvious.

It's a hornets' nest the size of a basketball, or bigger! "Crap!" I scream.

The customer's head is peering above the level of the attic floor.

I shout to him, "Get back, now!" I shimmy as fast as I can, carefully placing my knees on the two-inch joists. I feel another sting on my arm. I can't swat at it because I am using every limb for balance. I have to accept the stinger as a well-placed instrument of pain and warning from the hornet. Any error will cause me to fall through the drywall ceiling and into the master bedroom.

I make my escape, the adrenaline bringing my senses to heightened awareness. My feet land on the top of my ladder, and then I scurry down as fast as I can, tools clanging on the aluminum steps and falling out of their pouches, as if they are trying to escape the attack as well.

I grab the access panel and slide it closed as two of the menacing hornets fly past me.

In panic mode, the man is backing away. "I'm allergic! I'm allergic!"

He rushes out of the room, screaming and skipping steps as he runs down the carpeted stairs to the first floor.

I look for newspaper, but all I see is an envelope on his dresser. I use it to chase down the invaders and kill them.

Then I call down the steps, "It's okay; I got the ones that made it out."

The pain on my left arm is a nuisance, but bearable.

He is in the kitchen flipping pages, looking for an exterminator. I come around the corner and ask to use his sink to wash the wounds on my arm and neck.

"I can't live here like this!" he declares. "I can't sleep in that bed. They could have come through the ceiling in my sleep and killed me!"

My breathing is slowing down from my near-swarming. "I've seen a lot of things in attics—squirrels, opossums, rats, and mice," I admit, "but never that!"

He isn't paying attention to me. He's dialing the phone. "I have an emergency!" he says to the person on the other end.

While he is on the phone, I go back up to finish the wall plate. I look around me as I'm working, mindful that I may not have seen all the hornets that made it out.

"It's safe for now," I say from the top of the stairs.

The customer comes to the base of the steps with the phone at his ear. "Well, I'm not going back in there." There is fear in his voice. "Close the door ... wait ... could you get my cell phone and my pillows?" He is serious.

"Yeah, I'll get them." I retrieve his belongings and bring them down to the couch in the living room.

"They're coming this afternoon," he tells me. "I could have died!"

I am so glad that I am not allergic to stings, but my arm has a puffy, white bump.

His eyes are wide, and he is breathing erratically.

"Calm down; breathe through your nose; you'll be fine." I say it, but I know it's not helping him. A few minutes later, he is calling a friend and asking if he can stay with him for a few days.

"Sign here; I'm done," I say. He signs the paperwork with a shaking hand.

"Thank you," he says. "This is very serious for me. I am allergic to stings, and if I was stung, I could die." I respond, "No worries, sir. I'm glad you're okay."

Over the years, I have found that bees, wasps, and hornets show no mercy. I am thankful I was there and solved the mystery in his attic before it was too late.

Guess Who I Almost Ran Into

You never know what kind of person you will meet at your next appointment.

I was thinking about this as I looked down at the work order on my clipboard. *Mary Smith—what will she be like?* Coming to a four-way-stop intersection, I stop and wait my turn. I begin to pull out when a car coming from the other street does not stop. In fact, she turns in front of me and barely misses my right front fender.

Instinctively, I slam on my brakes and simultaneously honk my horn. The intersection is clearly marked, and she is definitely in a real hurry. My heart rate shoots up, and I am angry. I raise my hand as if to say, *What was that?*

Well, it happens. At least we didn't collide. I increase my speed and find myself on her tail. I must admit, I am getting too close. Then I think to myself, *It doesn't matter. She doesn't know me, and I don't know her.* I back off and allow the normal driving distance.

My GPS speaks up. "Left turn ahead." I see the car ahead of me turning left. I make the turn, too. Then my GPS says, "Turn right." Okay, I'll turn right. The same car is turning right ahead of me.

Now, I'm thinking, *I hope this crazy lady doesn't think I'm following her.* The housing development where I am going is just ahead. The GPS gives me more direction. "Turn right, then turn left at the second road." I look down at the screen and see the map, with the arrows pointing the way. The car I've been following since nearly having a wreck is making every turn I make. It's as though her GPS and mine are synced.

I am seriously hoping she isn't going to make the same turns, but sure enough, she does! *Is she watching my turn signals and anticipating my turns?*

This is so weird. Left, then right, right again, then left. Every move I make, she is making, but from a bird's-eye view, it would appear I am trailing her.

At the last turn, she rolls down her window and gives me an obscene gesture. *Sheesh, lady, you pulled out in front of me!*

The GPS states, "Your destination is three hundred feet on the left." She turns into the same driveway I am turning into!

I slow down; I am not sure what to do. *Do I keep driving, or do I keep my appointment?* I decide to pull in behind her.

She gets out of the car, slams the door, turns toward me, and with an avalanche of profanity, she lets me have it. "What do you think you're doing? You've got some nerve, following me the whole way home! Who do you think you are?"

Still in my van, I look down at the work order, check the address and the name, and ask, "Are you Mary Smith?" She'd been leaning forward in attack mode. Now surprised, she pulls her head back. "Yes, I am. How in the #$@% did you know that?"

I say in a professional tone, "I'm Dan, from the cable company, here to install your service."

Her mouth drops wide open. Inside, I'm laughing, but I raise my eyebrows like a teacher scolding a student.

"Oh!" she says in a low voice, "I thought you were stalking me."

I shake my head as I get out of my van. "Nope, I'm just following my GPS."

I can tell she's embarrassed. She says, "I was running late, and I didn't want to miss my appointment, so I guess I owe you an apology."

I let out a chuckle. "Well, I'll pretend the gesture you gave me a few turns ago was your way of saying, 'This way, we're almost there.'"

The tension breaks, and I do my job as usual.

To this day, when someone pulls out in front of me or cuts me off, I think, *Maybe he'll be my next customer.*

Doing Non-Pay Disconnects

One day, I was finished before noon. I had two cancellations, so I could have gone home, but I needed to make my goal, so I asked for more work. I was given seven non-pay disconnects.

Non-pay disconnects are when a customer does not pay their bill for two to three months. The idea is to knock on the door, ask for money, and leave.

Now, think about this: you are walking up to the door and interrupting whatever they may be doing and asking for money to keep their cable, Internet, or phone service on.

I learned years ago, after making some communication errors, just how to say things. I used to say, "Hi, I'm here from the cable company. You didn't pay your bill, so I am going to shut you off if you don't pay today."

Wow! If you want to make an enemy of a total stranger, this would be one way to do it. The negative words are filled with the implication of a threat. *You got no money, you got no cable!* It can really ruin your day when you draw out someone's anger and it becomes directed at you.

Over the years, I have perfected my line. Instead of saying, "You didn't pay," I say, "Apparently, they have not received your payment." See the difference?

Instead of saying, "I'm going to shut you off," I say, "If we can't collect the past balance, I will need to turn the service off."

Taking the subjective language out of the equation and

becoming more objective allows the customer to respond rather than react.

Using an apologetic tone does wonders. "I am so sorry to bother you. I'm from the cable company. There is a past-due balance that I need to collect today. If we could get this taken care of today, then I won't have to turn off the service."

Notice I didn't say "shut you off" or "turn you off." I'm not doing something *to* them. I am disconnecting something they use.

Yet, even with these nice words, I have been confronted with anger, frustration, and even physical threats to my body.

Most times, the response is embarrassment. I may even include, while they are writing the check, that I have been turned off myself. "So don't worry about," I'll say.

I have many stories about these encounters that would make almost anyone scamper away with her tail between her legs. Numerous accounts when words coming from their side of the door have made my spine tingle, and my right hand was buried in my pocket holding pepper spray.

I spoke with a policeman about non-pay disconnects. He said, "You are crazy. You have no idea what could happen in a situation like that! You are actually knocking on someone's door, asking for money, and then have the authority to disconnect their TV! You gotta have *cajones* for that!"

I must admit, there are times I have enjoyed it. I know ... shame on me. As I drive up to the house, I feel a light feeling in my chest. I know there could be a confrontation. I've done enough of them to be aware that anything could happen.

I look for clues. Are there any doors or windows open? Can they hear me? It may seem like I'm being sneaky, but I prefer to call it the art of stealth. If I park behind this tree and leave the truck running, maybe they won't see me coming, and I can leave quickly.

The worst part is putting up the ladder just outside their home, hearing the clanking noise of the twenty-eight-foot ladder as it clicks into place. I am wishing the ladder had a muffler.

Often in a city, I can actually see the TV on! I have even

watched a person get up from the couch during a commercial, and my opportunity presents itself. Disconnect quickly, terminate the port, watch the TV turn to snow, and let out an evil chuckle. Sometimes, I would do the villainous *bwahahaha* laugh, but not too loud. Then scurry like a mole to a hole.

Hearing a dog bark is a sign you might get caught in the act. *Stupid dog, shut up!* You're hoping the customer is not home or perhaps is asleep or out in the backyard. Then you lower the ladder, with that darn clanking noise as the rungs click downward. Throw it on your shoulder and hustle to get the beast onto the van and lock it in place before you are discovered.

My rearview mirror has seen the faces of many people looking out their front doors to the left and to the right, only to see my taillights getting smaller.

Yes, it's a nasty part of the job, and I've done thousands of them.

Bill Breslow was with me one day when a man leveled a shotgun at us while we ducked and drove away. Waiting for the buckshot to pummel the van, we kept our heads low and waited for the shattering of glass. It didn't happen.

Lots of things didn't happen that could have happened.

A man reached into his hoodie to pull out a gun, put it aside, and then handed me $200 for his past-due bill.

A baseball-bat carrying thug intentionally bumped into me from behind as I tried to collect money from his roommate.

I agreed to walk with a man down the block to get some money that someone owed him and then watched as a fistfight ensued. Needless to say, that collection didn't happen, and I went up the pole and turned off his cable. As I was putting my ladder on my van, he came running up to me, bloody-lipped, and said, "Please don't turn me off. I got some other money up the block. Come with me!"

I shook my head. "Sorry, buddy, I don't think you can take another beating."

Some companies preferred that you knock on the door and make an attempt, but then the world got more dangerous, and the cable companies got wiser. We can turn off their equipment. We still have to go up the poles, but we don't need to knock on the doors anymore.

When I think back on the years and the thousands of collections I've done, I shudder when I think of what could have happened.

One of my very first non-pay disconnects was in the city.

I had thirty of them to do that day, and I was feeling a bit overwhelmed. I was only twenty years old, just three months into my new job. My boss said, "Just knock on the door, show them the work order, and explain that you're there to collect what they owe. If they can't pay, just turn them off."

He said it in a matter-of-fact way, as though it were no big deal.

When doing a non-pay disconnect, there are several things that must be done at the pole. Cutting the fitting at the end of the wire is not one of them. What if they pay the next day? The next guy would have to take his entire tool belt up the pole to put a new fitting on.

So you twist off the connection and install a terminator on the port, and then screw the wire back on the terminator. That way, the fitting is still intact and the copper center conductor doesn't rust from the weather.

Even after you unscrew the cable, you still have a few details to take care of while you're twenty feet up in the air. What only takes a minute seems to take longer because you know that someone's TV just went to snow.

I knock on the door of a second-floor apartment. I'm nervous.

The door is opened abruptly. "Yeah? Who are you?"

The guy is about my age, but he's shorter. He's wearing jeans and a white T-shirt with the sleeves rolled up. He is solid muscle, and he's already agitated by my imposition.

"I'm here to collect for the cable. Can you pay it today?"

He drops his head an inch and stares at me. Looking right in my eyes without blinking, he says, "And?"

I am not sure what the *and* is for, so I ask, "And what?"

His head comes up level. He wags his tongue from one side of his open mouth to the other.

He answers slowly. "And what are you going to do if I don't have the money?" I can tell he's trying to scare me.

"If I don't collect, I have to disconnect." It just rolls off my tongue. I don't plan on saying it, but the rhyme is perfect and has a ring to it.

"You mean turn me off?" He's on to me.

I just say one word. "Yes."

He moves his hand off the doorknob and reaches up to hold the top of the door. I'm thinking he's trying to look taller. "Do what you got to do, man." He slams the door.

Out of his sight, I shrug my shoulders and go down the steps and outside to my van. I'm thinking, *That was easy.*

The ladder is up, and I'm climbing up the pole.

A window opens from his apartment and he yells, "You do that, man, and you'll be sorry!" I ignore him. My heart is pounding. I have never been in a confrontation like this. The window slams shut. I disconnect the cable.

Suddenly, I feel my ladder shaking. I hold on tight and look over my shoulder and down to the ground. There, at the base of my ladder, is the guy swinging a banister spindle from a stairwell. It resembles a bat, and he is using it to strike my ladder.

My strong fear turns to an equally matched anger.

He shouts up at me, "You better turn that back on, you &%#!" He is swearing at me and taunting me from below, striking the ladder with the rage of caged animal.

How I have the courage to act so tough, I will never know.

I come down the ladder about halfway and stop. He stands firm.

I don't raise my voice. I don't shout. My words are slow and deliberate. "Listen here, buddy," I say, "I've got way more weapons on me. My razor blade will cut you, and my screwdriver will stab you. You back off now, or you'll be the sorry one!"

The staring contest begins. What seems like a few minutes is probably just a few seconds. He mumbles an expletive and walks away. I stay in my position halfway up the ladder until he enters the apartment building.

As soon as I estimate how long it will take to get down and mount the ladder on my van, I scramble like a chicken running from a fox.

I was terrified. It was actually a good thing that it happened on my first day. From then on, I realized that doing this kind of work in the cable industry takes a bit of strategy, courage, and toughness I didn't know I had.

I knock on the door to collect—or to disconnect the cable.

The small front porch has crushed beer cans strewn about. A white, plastic lawn chair sits three feet from the door, with a milk crate for a table.

On it is an ashtray spilling over with smashed cigarette butts, of which a few had fallen while lit and burned the outdoor carpet. The windows are shaded with a film of cigarette smoke. I hear a dog barking.

Then I hear the footsteps. I step back to allow the screen door to open. My head, which is level, begins to slowly rise as I see a massive man. He is wearing "colors"—the jacket that bears the name of the outlaw motorcycle gang he is a member of. His neck has a front-to-back ring of four-inch tattoos: daggers, with blood dripping from the points.

"Here to collect for the cable," I say with trepidation.

"You're here for what?"

I know I'm in for a bit of an adventure. "I ... um ... have to collect for the cable. It hasn't been paid for a few months." I am six feet tall with my boots on, but this monster seems a foot taller. I am nervous.

"I don't have it," he says. "Go away."

I don't want to just walk away. I have to tell him of the consequence. "Uh, sir, if I don't collect, I have to turn off the cable."

I shut up and let it process in his brain as he is staring at me.

"So, what you're telling me is that if I don't pay you, you're going to go up that pole, right in front of me, and turn my cable off."

He nailed it! I take a deep breath. "Yes."

He is staring me down. Then he asks, "What's your name?" I never had anyone ask that. "Dan Armstrong."

He looks at me and repeats my name back to me, "Dan Armstrong." It's as though he is going to remember me. *Why didn't I say* Edwin Markle! No, I had to give him my *real* name!

I feel like I have to defend myself. "Sir, I'm just doing my job. It's nothing personal, believe me!"

There's an awkward silence, like a face-off. He knows I can do what I am there to do, but, I think, he also knows I am intimidated by him.

I try not to show it. I try to look neutral, but I'm lousy at poker.

He starts nodding and clenching his sharp jaw. "Hold on. I got to put the dog away. Don't do anything." He closes the door.

Well, I wasn't about to do anything. What I want to do is walk quietly off the porch, run down the sidewalk to my van, and get the heck out of there.

I wait. The door opens again, and this time, he steps back into his living room. "C'mon in," he says in a voice that I recognize as a welcome.

I step inside the house. His motorcycle is parked in the living room. He is changing the oil. On the carpet!

The TV is on. I look over at it, wishing at this moment that he had not answered, that maybe he would have been in the bathroom and come back downstairs to his project to hear static on the TV.

Too late now. I'm standing in his house, waiting for payment. He retrieves a check and writes out the amount he owes. I hand him my clipboard to sign for his receipt. My clipboard looks like a small pad in his hands. It appears to have shrunk in the transfer of hands.

I give him a receipt and turn to walk out the door. "Have a good day, sir," I say as I am opening the door to leave.

"Hey," he says in a gruff voice, "thanks for knocking." He sounds sincere.

I turn back to look at him. "You're welcome."

Later, feeling safe in my locked van, I think, *I have to come up with a better fictitious name!*

I Have What I Need, Thanks

You never know what you're going to see when that door opens.

I knock on the door and take a deep breath. It's a normal habit of mine. I want to appear calm. Or perhaps I do it to prepare me for the strange, the bizarre, the surprise just behind the door.

A man answers. The first thing that catches my eye is what looks like a long Band-Aid on his forehead. It's not. It's a strip of double-stick tape, arching across his forehead from one side to the other. I also notice another strip running from the middle of the forehead strip back over the top of his balding head. It's in the shape of an upside-down *T*.

After this quick glance, I act as if I haven't noticed. Pretty quickly, I figure out what it is. It's preparation for donning his toupee.

"What are we doing today?" I ask.

"I want a TV in my bedroom, but you may have a problem."

I've come to realize that when some people say this, it's simply because they don't understand how to run cable. In their mind, it may be impossible.

"What problem might I have?" I'm curious, and I want to resolve his concerns as soon as possible.

"Let me show you." He gestures for me to follow him.

As we walk down a long hallway, he points to each door. "That's my son's room; that's my storage room; that's the bathroom; that's a closet; and here we are. My room!"

The room is chaotic—unkempt bed, a pile of papers on top of

a dusty dresser, ratty carpets with chewing-tobacco stains, and his TV in the corner, sitting on a rolling shelf designed for a much lighter load.

"So, what's the problem?" I ask. I haven't seen anything that causes me concern.

"Well, you see, the TV is here in my room, but the cable comes in on the other side of the house." He pauses, as if I understand what he's intimating. I remain quiet, hoping he will tell me more.

"You see, from this corner of the house to the other corner of the house is pretty far!" I'm still not sure what he's trying to tell me, so I begin to ask my usual questions.

"Do you have a basement?"

"Yes."

"Good. Does it have a drop ceiling or drywall?"

"Nope. It's just the rafters."

I turn to leave the room. "Okay, let's go look."

I lead him back through The Hall of Designated Doorways. I find the basement door in the kitchen and begin to open it.

"Wait a minute," he says. "You'll need this."

He hands me a broom. I don't ask why. I just accept that there is a reason this guy is handing me a broom.

"It's for the cobwebs," he says. "I haven't been down there for a long time, and it's really bad."

We reach the basement. Except for the smell of spilled fuel oil mixed with mildew, it isn't that bad. Don't misunderstand me; I wouldn't want to throw a party down there, but I've seen worse.

The broom comes in handy. With the spiderwebs wrapped around the bristles, the broom looks like a giant stick of cotton candy. The customer follows the path I'm clearing, staying a few feet back to avoid death by broomstick. And to avoid getting cobwebs stuck to the tape on his head.

We make our way back to the corner of the basement, directly below where his TV sits in his bedroom.

He speaks up. "You see, the TV is right above our heads, and the cable comes in *the whole way down there*." It sounds like he's singing a country song, the way he says "the whoooole waaaaay downnn theerrre."

When he's finished singing, I ask, "So, what's the problem? It's a clear path, and the splitter is right there. The line is probably fifty feet at the most."

He sighs. "You see, that's the problem. That's a long way to go, and I don't have the wire for it."

My mind is racing with things I want to say. Things like, *Why did you call me here today if you think I don't have cable wire?* Or, *Yeah, I should have stopped at Wal-mart before I came here.* I resist the temptation.

He jumps on my pause. "Do you have cable on your truck?"

The customer is asking if the cable guy, who is coming to his house to install cable, *has cable?*

I smile and reply, "I have a roll of cable in my truck that's a thousand feet long. I think I have enough." He lets out a sigh of relief.

"Whew, that's good. Do you have a drill?"

Is this guy serious? "Yes, sir, I have a drill."

He nods approvingly.

"So, you've done this before, huh?"

I smile again. "Yeah, I've been doing this for quite a while."

He smiles, reaches up, puts his hand on my shoulder, and says, "I bet you meet some crazy people too, huh?

"Oh, sir, you have *no* idea.

Roy Gilley's Story

While training a new guy, I find myself telling stories as we drive between appointments—stories of chickens in the basement or of being threatened by non-paying customers about to have their cable turned off.

Roy was now ready to be on his own.

On his first day, I reminded him, "Remember your training, relax, and keep in mind, you will find yourself in situations that my training could not possibly prepare you for."

I knew it wouldn't be long until Roy had a story.

My cell phone rings. "Hey, Dan, it's Roy."

"Yeah, Roy, what's up?"

"Oh, Dan, I got a story!"

I laugh and ask, "What is it?"

Roy can hardly contain himself at first as he proceeds to tell me his adventure.

"I knocked on this door, and a very short Chinese lady answered." He pauses.

"How did you know she was Chinese?" I ask.

"I knew you would ask that, Dan. She had a paper pinned to her dress that said, 'I am Chinese and do not understand English. Please speak into this tablet.' She held up a device and I spoke into it: 'I am the cable guy here to put in your cable.'"

"You're kidding me, Roy!"

"I kid you not! But as soon as I said it, I heard a voice. It was her son in Chicago. He told me to ask him the questions, then he would ask her in Chinese and translate back to me in English so I could do the installation."

"That's amazing, Roy! How long did that all take?"

"I'm not sure just yet. I had to step outside to tell you. I'm just so excited that I have a cable story now!"

My Encounter with Lucifer

Dogs are fascinating animals.

Some of them are so timid, they run for cover as soon as you enter the house. Other pooches think you're there just to see them, and they shower you with loving affection.

Then there are those dogs that see you as a threat, despite their owners' words of assurance.

I knock on the door, and this dog shows that he intends to protect his home. He is jumping on the door, barking, and growling, in no small way making sure I know he is not going to let me in.

Through the door, I hear the sentence I've heard a thousand times: "Hold on, let me put the dog away."

A few minutes later, the door opens, and a small-framed girl in her mid-twenties greets me.

"I'm sorry. We used to put him outside on a chain, but he keeps breaking them." The dog is a black Rottweiler, a huge animal with incredible power. I don't know where she's put the beast, but I'm safe for now.

She shows me the two rooms where she wants the TVs connected. Both must be installed by drilling through the floor into the basement. A problem presents itself.

The dog is in the basement.

"Can he be put in another room?" I ask.

"No. I barely got him down there. I had to throw a raw hamburger down the steps so he would chase it."

Uh-oh. "Here's my plan. I drill the holes and push down enough wire for where they need to go. Can you hold him while I work?"

"I think so."

"You think so? I need you to know so." Now I am wondering why we can't just reschedule this installation twelve years from now, when the dog has passed on to doggy heaven.

We proceed with the plan. I drill the holes and feed plenty of wire through them into the unfinished basement. The dog is barking ferociously at what he might be thinking are thin black snakes.

I say to the girl, "Okay, ready to go?"

She takes a deep breath. "Ready as I'll ever be!"

She cracks open the basement door, and in a sweet, high-pitched voice, she calls out, "Luuuu-ci-ferrr ..."

Lucifer. What an appropriate name.

The dog charges up the steps, and the young lady leaps into action. I slam the door behind her to protect myself.

From the other side of the door, I hear a cacophony of tools clanging together and hitting the floor, cans falling from shelves, bodies tangled in combat, snarling and growling, grunting and moaning.

Then silence.

For a few seconds, I ponder the girl's fate. Had I sent her to her doom? Had she fallen and Lucifer decided that suppertime had come early?

I crack the door open, putting my foot against the base to prevent Lucifer from charging through. I don't want to be his dessert.

I call out in a soft voice, "Hello? Are you okay?"

I imagine Lucifer licking his fangs, looking up from his prey, and snickering to himself. *I hope that stupid cable guy comes down here.*

A moment passes. Then I hear the young woman. Her voice is strained. "Are you coming?"

"Do you have him?" I ask.

"Yes! Both of my hands have his collar."

There's no switch at the top of the stairs, no lights to show me what I'm up against.

I inch down the creaking wooden steps, giving away my presence to Lucifer. I'm descending into *his* world, and he is about to let me know it. It's tough enough to *work* in the dark with just a tiny flashlight, but being stalked by a 150-pound, manic Rottweiler is almost too much to deal with.

Now aware of my presence, Lucifer lunges toward me, dragging the petite lady several feet within a second. She yanks back on the collar and cries out, "*Lucifer!*"

His snarling jaws are wide with fury, his teeth gleaming, his eyes reddened by my flashlight. I can no longer see the girl. Lucifer's body obscures my view of her completely; the dog is taller and wider than she is. All I have is her voice to let me know that she's still here, in the darkness of this hole.

I yell to her in anger, "Are you *sure* you can hold him?"

"Hurry!" She strains as Lucifer stands on his hind legs like a mama bear protecting her cubs. "He's really strong!"

As I quickly locate the wires that dangle through the holes I've drilled, a beam of sunlight catches my eye. The light shows me an opening in the foundation where a few rocks have fallen out. I use the crevice to my advantage and quickly fish the wires to the outside.

I turn to see Lucifer gaining ground. The girl's chokehold keeps him from barking, but he is walking on his hind legs. He takes one step, then another. When she cries, "I can't hold him anymore!" I begin to fear for my life. Lucifer has pulled the young woman at least ten feet, her shoes scraping and sliding along the concrete.

Somehow, I calculate her strength compared to his. I decide I have about three seconds to get to the base of the steps before Lucifer achieves his goal and eats the cable guy.

I dash to the stairs and start scrambling up, using my hands and legs for momentum, tools spilling out of my tool belt. "Crap!" I shout. Lucifer, still on two legs, makes his way closer. Now *I'm* the animal running for its life.

I hit the door with my head, and the door swings open. Spinning around, I reach for the door and slam it shut behind me. I throw my back against it and slide down to the floor.

Catching my breath, I start to laugh, thinking to myself, *That was crazy! Who keeps a dog like that?*

Once I can breathe enough to talk, I shout through the door, "You okay?"

Lucifer is barking now, so I can't hear a word. I call out again. "I'm going outside. Why don't you come up and shut the door, then call me back in when it's safe!"

I hear her yell back in a space between the barks, "'Kay!"

A minute passes. Then the front door opens and she calls for me.

I ask, "Is Lucifer still in the basement?"

"Yeah, I threw him some more meat. He'll be all right for a while. Just keep your voice down so he thinks you left."

I nod in total agreement. "By the way, I lost a screwdriver and a wrench down there ..." Before I finish my sentence, she asks, "Do you want to go get them?"

I smirk. "Are you kidding me? If my pants had fallen off, I wouldn't go get them. I'd walk out of here in my underwear, soiled and all!"

She laughed. I didn't.

"Yeah, we can't chain him outside anymore. He's broken every chain, and he's pulled out fence posts. He's even hauled a railroad tie out to the road."

I am not amused. "Maybe it's none of my business, but he could hurt somebody."

She looks me dead in the face and says, "He's trained to kill, and that's what he'll do if someone breaks in this house. And you're right. It's none of your business."

I complete the installation outside, and she signs the work order without a word.

As I drive away, I look back and see Lucifer standing up at the front door, front paws stretched up high. I'm sure he's grinning through the glass. I know what he's thinking. *Next time, cable guy, you're mine!*

That's Okay; Keep It

She answers the door looking frazzled and holding a two-year-old girl. Another two-year-old clings to her leg.

"Hi, I'm Dan. I'm here to install a high-definition recorder box. Is that right?"

She opens the door wider so I can squeeze past the three-person welcome committee.

"Come on in. I'm running a daycare here. Three grandchildren!"

I laugh. The girl she's holding is burying her head in her grandmother's neck, and the other is dragging her feet as her grandmother shuffles to the living room.

The customer points with her free hand. "There it is. We've been wanting to get this done since buying this monster." She's referring to the sixty-inch flat-screen TV in the corner.

I go about my business hooking up the box, and I hear the grandmother ask one of the two-year-olds, "Do you have to use the bathroom?"

The little girl is looking up from the floor and simply raises her arms high. "Hold me!"

The grandmother rolls her eyes and says, "Let me put your cousin down first."

She lowers one child to the floor and lifts up the other.

"Are you sure you don't have to use the bathroom?" she asks the toddler again. The little girl snuggles in close, ignoring the question.

I am now finished hooking up the box and programming the

remote, and I say, "Are you ready for a lesson on how to use the remote?"

"Let me sit down," the woman says. She sits on a chair, and I squat down beside her to show her the remote. The toddler continues wrapping her limbs around her grandmother.

"So here's how it works," I say, launching into my five-minute lesson on recording, pausing live TV, using the guide, the information button, on and off, and so forth.

Finally, I finish and hold out my pen and clipboard for her signature. The customer unwraps her hand from her granddaughter, takes the pen as I hold the clipboard, and begins to sign.

Suddenly, she cries, "Oh, no!"

I'm not sure why there would be a problem, so I ask, "Is it the name? Isn't it spelled right?"

Grandmother says, "No, that's not it. My little princess here peed all over me, and my hands are soaked with pee."

"That's okay," I say. "You can keep the pen."

Things That Go Bump in the Afternoon

When you work for a small cable company, there are times when you install at houses that are side by side.

I have done installs on the same street for days at a time. So it's not uncommon for the customer to know something about your next appointment before you go there.

In this case, it was *after* an appointment that I learned something about where I'd just been.

The first appointment was at a trailer. On either side of this lot were well-kept yards, with shrubbery defining the property lines. The decorative mailboxes and pristine walkways were bookends for this middle lot, which made it look worse. The grass was high. It would take a weed whacker or a few goats to get the grass low enough for a lawnmower.

I knocked on the flimsy door. A young man answered. "Come on in."

It was dark, but soon my eyes adjusted. Dry aquariums lined a wall.

"What's in the cages?" I asked.

"Oh, they're my snakes."

I nodded. "Three cages, three snakes?"

"No. The third cage is their dinner." I saw movement when he turned on a small lamp. A few small mice scrambled for cover.

"Well, where do you want the cable?"

He showed me two locations. He wanted one in the living room and one in the bedroom. The living room TV was in the middle of the trailer, at the kitchen wall.

Crap! I thought. It's always easier to drill down at the edge of an outside wall when doing a trailer install. By doing this, you need only to remove the skirting by sliding it upward, reach under for the cable and throw it over a few feet. You then remove another section of skirting, pull some more cable, and continue that way until you have all the wiring to a central location.

"Are you sure you want it here?" I suggested a different location so I wouldn't have to crawl twelve feet under a trailer. "Maybe if you put it here by the window, you can watch the TV and see who comes up to the front, too."

He paused for a second. "No, I want it here."

I pursed my lips. "Okay, you're the boss," I said.

I went outside and got my drill and cable reel. I use a straightened metal coat hanger to attach the cable to. When I crawl under a trailer, the coat hanger will pierce through the insulation, making the cable easier to find.

This particular trailer was old. The skirting was cracked, and quite a few pieces were missing. I removed the piece that lined up with the place I drilled and began my crawl. Dead spiders, coated in some kind of white foam, hung suspended by webs. Insulation, drooping from years of condensation from the air conditioner unit, slid over my back as I crawled like a soldier in basic training. The weak flashlight in my mouth lit only the space right in front of me, but I spotted the protruding coat hanger and made the grab.

Suddenly, I felt a chill run up my spine. I felt like I was being watched.

Then something touched my boot.

Still lying on my stomach, I turned quickly. Nothing there. *Must be the insulation dropping,* I told myself.

I wriggled my body around in a half-circle to crawl out. The open skirting revealed the natural light. I turned the flashlight off to save the batteries. I came out from underneath the trailer, got up to my knees, and then stood. I turned around and pulled the length of cable I needed.

"Tight squeeze?" It was the customer's voice.

"Yeah. And dark." I began to slide the skirting into place.

"What's it like under there?" the young man asked.

I brushed the dirt off my knees. "I wouldn't put a third bedroom in there," I said, grinning. Since the job was finished, I had him sign the paperwork.

"Have a good day!" I said and got into my van.

The next work order was for next door. I pulled in the driveway. A well-manicured lawn bordered the trailer property. The line was distinct because of the difference in the height of the grass.

The man came out and said, "I saw you next door. Did you see a snake?"

I usually don't talk about other installations, especially next door. It's really not their business, but this time I did.

"Yeah, he's got a few of them in cages."

The man shook his head. "No, no, no. I'm not talking about inside, I'm talking about the ten-foot corn snake that lives *under* his trailer!"

Instantly, bumps rose on my arms like ants on a tree limb.

"*What*?" I exclaimed.

"That darn snake comes over into my yard and suns himself. I have even run over him with my mower by accident, and he just slides away like it's nothing."

At this point, I was almost freaking out.

He continued, "Yeah, that darn snake lives under his trailer. I saw you crawl under there and I was wondering if you saw it."

I replied, "I am *so* glad I installed *him* first and *not you!*"

"Does Your Dog Bite?"

It's a question I ask at least once a day. The sound of knocking or a ringing doorbell often sets off a torrent of vicious barking.

The dog on the other side of this door is intimidating, to say the least. I hear a voice from inside. "Give me a minute. I'll put the dog away."

The creature is barking and jumping up at the glass panels of the front door. His breath is hot enough to steam the windows. His lips curl back, exposing his sharp, white teeth. *The better to eat you with, my dear.*

The customer calls the killer dog, and the animal turns from the door and follows his owner. Then, for whatever reason, the dog turns and looks back at me. He faces the door again, barks once, and then begins to charge. The homeowner yells, but the dog is intent on protecting, and I am the threat. Through the window, I see the beast bounding toward me.

The door between us is my only defense, but it's a strong one.

Or so I think.

I take a step back as I see the dog leap up. He disappears for a moment, and then suddenly, his paws make contact with the glass panels of the door. The glass shatters and jagged little missiles shoot out in my direction. My eyes instinctively close and my hands start to rise, but it's too late. A few of the shards hit me in the face, cutting me on my cheek and forehead.

The animal pulls his paws out from the window frame. Blood trails him as he trots away. The homeowner grabs him by the neck and pulls him away. After putting the dog into another room, he slams the door.

I have already retreated to my van to look for my first aid kit. I want to put pressure on the cuts. I only find napkins.

The customer is apologizing as he is running toward my van. I'm sitting in the driver's seat, looking up at the rearview mirror, dabbing at my cuts.

"Are you okay?" the man asks.

I acknowledge his question as I tend to my wounds. "Yeah, I'm fine. I'm just shaken up a bit. Does your dog bite?"

"Oh, he might nip ya a little bit, but he ain't killt nobody yet."

As I apply pressure to the cuts on my forehead, I say, "Can you put him in a locked room so I can work without feeling threatened?"

The man nods and thinks for a second. "I could put him in the basement, but you'll need to go down there, won't you?"

I nod.

"Hmmm. I have an idea!" the man says. "I'll hold him while you work."

I *tsk* three times and respond, "Nope. He needs to be put in a room I won't need to go into, like the bathroom. Or tie him up outside."

The man replies, "Nope. He can jump any fence, so that's not happening. And I'm not putting him in the bathroom for that long."

I'm surprised at what he's saying. "It's my dog, my house, and I'm not going to make it hard on my dog."

I need a moment to calm myself, so I take a slow, deep breath through my nose and then let it out again.

"Sir, when you want your cable installed, call us when the dog is secure; otherwise, we are not putting ourselves in danger."

I start my van. He backs away, and I drive off.

As far as I know, no one went back to install his cable.

I just hope the satellite guy had better luck.

Not Cool, Mom

There's a policy that people in my profession adhere to: do not enter a house if the only person there is under eighteen. It's not a question you want to ask when the door opens, but sometimes it's obvious.

A young teenage boy answers the door. I introduce myself.

"Hi, I'm Dan from the cable company. Are your parents home?"

The boy steps back and waves me in. "Yeah, my mom's upstairs in her room. She told me to tell you that we are hooking up the TV here in the living room and the one in the basement." There's no reason not to believe him, so I enter and go to work.

About forty-five minutes later, I'm finished. It occurs to me that "Mom" never showed her face. I come upstairs from the basement and pull out the clipboard.

"Okay, young man, I need your mom to sign this." He reaches for the clipboard, but I pull it back just enough to show that I'm not handing it to him. I want his mother to sign it here, now, in front of me.

The kid looks nervous. I say, "Could you go get your mom for me?" His eyes are shifting, and he's trying to think of something to say. I say, "If you can take me upstairs, she can sign it there. Okay?"

He's stuck. He has to tell the truth. "My mom's not here."

Disgusted with his answer, I ask, "How old are you?"

He shrinks back. "Thirteen."

Shaking my head, I look at him like a dad to a young son. "You know, you have me in a bad spot here. I can get into a lot of trouble. Where is your mom?"

He is embarrassed and replies, "She's at work, and she told me to tell you that she was up in bed. She said the cable can't be turned on without an adult here, so she asked me to lie. So we could get the cable."

I sigh deeply and walk out the door. I turn around and face him.

"Listen, son, I'm going to call the company right now and tell them what happened here. Do not be surprised if they tell me to turn the cable off. Understand?"

He nods his head and closes the door.

The company documents my story as I detail it to them, and they tell me to promptly disconnect the service.

This scenario has happened several times since this particular occasion.

I am the wiser now. Now I ask for the parent or grandparent, and a few times, I have asked to see some form of ID when a young person answered the door. I've learned to be very careful.

Roach Motels

Veteran cable installer Tom Lander and I were swapping stories as I helped him on an installation.

"Did you ever hear my cockroach story?" he asked.

"No, I haven't! But I would love to!"

Tom began. "I got a service call at this apartment to replace two bad digital boxes. I pulled in the driveway and there was a guy passed out in a car. I didn't give him much thought because of the area I was in.

"I knocked on the door and there's no answer. Then it occurred to me that maybe the guy in the car was the customer. So, I walk over to the window and tap on the glass. The guy jerks awake and looks up at me. I ask if he lives here and was he expecting us. The guy says, 'Yeah.'

"When I walked in the door, the smell overwhelmed me. The guy shows me the cable boxes that are bad and when I go to pick them up, a swarm of cockroaches scatters."

Tom looked down and shook his head, obviously reliving the moment.

"Ugh, I can't believe this guy," he said. "He wants me to put these things in my truck. No way, ain't gonna happen. So I told the guy that he has to bag them up and bring them in himself. The guy looks at me and says, 'Aren't you going to replace these today?'"

Tom cracked a sly smile and continued, "I told the guy, 'I am not going to take out these two boxes and replace them with two more that you're going to mess up.' So I called my supervisor and told him what was going on. The boss told me to inform the customer that the only way we will give him this type of service is if he provides a receipt from an extermination company."

My head popped back. "Seriously?"

Tom chuckled and said, "Yeah! Why should we put our equipment in a house like that, knowing we're going to have the same problem again?"

I must say, I was impressed at the wisdom of this particular case. "So what happened? Did the guy do it?" I asked.

Tom responded, "Don't know. I never heard any more about it. So, as far as we know, this guy having cockroaches as pets was far more valuable than watching his favorite TV shows."

Window Shudders

I love British accents; they intrigue me. And they're fun to listen to.

I meet many people, and the accents I hear from all over the world interest me. I always want to know what brought them to the States, how long they've been here, and whether they like it.

The customer speaks with an accent, so of course I ask him, "Where are you from?"

He stands erect, throws his chest out with pride, and with much dignity, answers, "Manchester, England."

We chat, and then it's time for me to get started running a line to his house. He goes inside as I make my way back to my van.

A moment later, he pops his head out the door and calls to me, "Would you like a hot beverage on this chilly day? Tea ...?" He pauses and raises his eyebrows, fully expecting me to jump at his offer of English hospitality. "Or perhaps coffee?"

I'm not a huge tea drinker. "Coffee."

His eyebrows settle down; his expectant smile is replaced with a grimace. I barely hear him as he mutters, "Typical American."

A few minutes later, as I'm propping my ladder against the house, he comes outside carrying a travel mug with the small sip-hole open. I can see wisps of steam rising and dissipating in the cold air. He sets a plate of small Christmas cookies beside it. "Here's your joe and a plate of crackers."

As I'm beginning to climb, I look down at the treats. "Thank you! You didn't have to do that."

"No problem, chap," he says with a gesture.

I come down for a quick sip. I pop a cookie in my mouth, and then it's gloves back on and up the cold fiberglass ladder. The Englishman walks inside, and as I begin my work, I see the curtain at the window being pulled aside.

With the cable now attached to the house, I move my ladder to a pole and walk back to throw the cable line through a tree. Once it's above the limbs, I pull up the slack and attach the cable to the pole.

One more pole to go. To get to this one, I have to cross the road and a small stream. I carry the ladder on my shoulder and skip over the stream with one hop. Once my ladder is at the final pole, I pull up the cable so it doesn't sag too low across the road.

Looking back at the house, I notice the curtain being pulled back again. I'm probably two hundred feet from the house, but I can see the figure of a man standing there in the window. Above him is a second window. That curtain is also open, and I see a figure in white.

How about that? I think to myself. *An audience.* I finish the connection and decide to leave my ladder at the pole. It will be easier to drive to it when I leave rather than walk two hundred feet with an extension ladder balanced on my shoulder.

As I walk back, I glance at the house and see the curtain fall back into place. The second-floor window curtain is still drawn, and the figure dressed in white is still there.

I walk in the front door and the customer says, "You're quite the brute, carrying that ladder all that way and jumping over the culvert like that."

I laugh and say, "Once you balance the ladder, it's really nothing."

"Interesting," he says. "This whole process of watching a wire go up from the house to the pole was quite entertaining. This house was built in 1825 and served as servants' quarters before the Civil War. To imagine that this house now has this sort of technology is fascinating to me. I hope you don't mind me watching you?"

I reply, "I don't care. The person on the second floor watched me the whole time, too."

His smile disappears. "*What* did you say?"

"The person upstairs, he was watching me too."

He tilts his head and looks at me over his glasses. "No one else lives here but me. *What did you see?*"

I stop working and look up at him. Chills ripple from my shoulders into my neck.

"*Seriously*, sir?"

He stands there, silent and still. Ten seconds pass. I'm holding my breath.

Suddenly, he breaks out in laughter. "Got you, didn't I?"

With a sudden sigh of relief, I mutter, "Uh ... yeah?"

He removes his spectacles as though he's about to make a profound point. "It's a mannequin, old boy. It scares the hell out of people. Better than a watchdog, eh?"

He is laughing now, and I am relieved. Typical Englishman.

The Psychic

Some of the distinctive architecture in West Chester, Pennsylvania, was designed more than a hundred years ago. Quaint streets dotted with small shops and cafes invite you to stay and visit awhile. I really enjoyed my time in that town, installing cable at West Chester University, in shops, and in apartments above businesses.

One place in particular still stands out in my memory.

The sign on the small shop on Gay Street said, "Psychic, Tarot Card Reader," followed by the name of the psychic. The door beside it led to the second-floor studio apartment, where the owner lived.

I climbed the stairs and knocked on the door.

The woman yelled from behind the door, "Who is it?"

I said, "Why don't you tell me, if you're able?" I was having fun.

"What?" she grunted.

I didn't want to make trouble, so I answered a little louder, "I'm here to install your cable."

She should have known, for two reasons.

Number one: she made the appointment.

Number two: she was a psychic.

Must have been her day off.

The Cats Owned the Place

As I stand at the front door of the mobile home, my sniffer immediately recognizes the smell. Cats!

Entering a house with pets is always a challenge. Being careful not to let the cat out while going in and out the door takes extra time. Quite honestly, it's frustrating.

This particular home is a cat trailer. I immediately notice a small village of little houses mounted on a long shelf in the living room. A ramp starts at the floor and leads up to the shelf. The houses are for the cats. It seems to me that the perch gives the felines a feeling of mastery over their domain.

"How many cats do you have?" I ask. "I want to make sure the three or four I see scurrying around don't dart out the door." I want to be sensitive.

"Oh, we have sixteen ... no, wait, seventeen. I always forget."

Dishes of food are everywhere. I have to play hopscotch in order to miss the plastic land mines. Plates of food lie on the countertops, the kitchen table, and every available shelf. Overflowing litter boxes sit side by side in the kitchen. Yes, in the kitchen.

"Wow!" I exclaim. "I'll be careful when I use the door so they don't sneak out."

The lady smiles. "Oh, no. I wouldn't want that. They have never been outside."

My eyes grow wide. "Never? They've never been outside?"

She looks around at the furry critters. "No. They have all been declawed, and they all were born inside."

The smell is impossible to ignore. I've been in houses with several cats and didn't notice any odor, but this house is anathema to my nostrils. Every breath is a chore. I have to be careful not to breathe in too deeply. The ammonia is already burning my eyes.

She shows me where everything is to go, and I get started.

When I finish, I find her sitting in her chair. Two cats lie on top of the chair back, and one lies on her lap as she caresses it. The cat is purring loudly, and I don't want to startle it.

"Ma'am, I'm going to kneel down here beside you and show you how the remote works." I kneel down, and the kitty flips over and jumps off her lap.

"She doesn't know you. That's why she jumped that fast. Most of them are afraid of men, so don't take it personally."

I laugh. "Oh, I won't." I put both of my knees down and place the remote in her hands. "Okay, this is the power button. This is the volume button. This is the channel button ..."

As I'm describing each feature on the remote, I begin to feel a warm sensation on my knees. I continue, "Now, this is the guide button, and this one here is the menu button."

It's a cold day, and I'm wearing khakis with sweatpants underneath. The warm feeling on my knees is spreading as the weight of my body presses me down into the carpet.

I pause during my instruction and stand up. I look down at my knees, and both of them are wet. Not thinking, I run my hands over my knees to brush them off, and my hands pick up the dampness. I bring my hands up to my face, and I smell the strong odor of cat urine. I had been kneeling in cat pee and it soaked through my pants, into my sweatpants, and onto my skin. It doesn't take long until I feel the skin on my knees burning from the liquid that has seeped through my pants.

"Sign here," I demand.

She takes my clipboard and signs the work order, and I flee out of the trailer. I quickly find some hand wipes in my van and scrub my knees. The sanitized wipes turn yellow as I ferociously rub the splotches of urine. It's all over my hands and my clothing.

I start my van and drive away. I am an hour from home with many more appointments, and there is no time to go home and change my clothing. I turn on the heat in the van as I drive, and the urine smell begins filling my vehicle. I roll down the windows, but to no avail; the stench is permeating the interior. The heat in my van is causing the urine to smell worse. I pull my van over and scrub my knees again.

I think I've eliminated the smell—until I arrive at my next customer's house. While I'm working, she sniffs a couple of times and asks me, "Do you smell that?"

I shrug. "Maybe it's your plumbing."

That experience taught me this: when working in a house full of cats, Do Not Kneel.

Please, Sir, Don't Cry!

I was training a new recruit. We were going into an elderly man's house to install a box. He wanted to have a few more channels, and he was sold on the idea that the box was the answer.

We knocked on the door. The first question at the door from the old man was, "Do I have to have a new remote?"

Caught off guard from the beginning, I said, "Let's have a look."

He seemed placated by my response. He kindly allowed us in, and I proceeded to hook up the new digital box. I figured that by the time I was done, he would have warmed up to me and would trust that I would teach him well.

The entire time I was making the connection, he was standing over my shoulder, watching every move I made. I backed up and bumped into him when I was finished. "Oh, excuse me," I said. "Why don't you sit here on your chair and I'll explain," here it came, "the new remote!"

I didn't scream it. I calmly stated it.

But I think what he heard was something like a dreadful sound in a tunnel, with a bright light approaching him at lightning speed. His hands gripped the armrests. He looked like he was afraid of a drill and I was a dentist. His eyes widened and his mouth opened slightly. I was pretty sure I heard a soft moan.

I started. "This is your new remote. It's really easy to operate. You'll really like it!" I said it all cheerfully and with a caring smile. The old man looked down at the remote in my hand and back up at me. I felt like a mother trying to feed a baby a spoonful of asparagus! He looked horrified and, in a strange way, defiant. Like a toddler saying no to his mommy, he said, "I don't want a new remote!"

"Now, sir, you have to have a new remote. It'll be good for you. You'll like it."

Well, I wasn't going to force-feed him, so I began slowly.

"Look, this is your old remote." I held it in my hand and he reached for it. "No, no. This remote is going to be put away. The new remote is your friend."

I looked at him with a little more authority and firmness. I continued, "This new remote operates the digital box and the TV. It changes the channels on the box and changes the volume on the TV. Only one remote is needed."

I nodded my head and looked for his agreement. "You have to leave your TV on channel 3 and then change your channels from the digital box, okay?"

The old man's brow was furrowed with confusion. "I don't understand. My TV stays on channel 3. I rarely watch channel 3."

"Okay, you can watch any channel you want—*from the digital box*. What's your favorite channel?"

He said, "Channel 8 is my favorite."

"Great! All you have to do is press 8 on this remote." I said it slowly and pointed deliberately at the new remote.

"Where is it?" he asked frantically.

"It's right there," I said, pointing to the keypad. "It's marked with an *8*."

"I don't like this!" The old man was visibly shaken by this new technology in his hand. I thought, *Where did I go wrong?*

I spoke again. "Let's start over. Before, you used your TV remote to change the channels, but now you want more channels, so in order for you to get the channels you want, we use this remote to change the channels, because the new channels are on the digital box and not the TV."

My trainee was standing there, his eyes wide and unblinking. He told me later that he would not have known what to do.

The man started to pout, like a baby ready to cry.

And then he did. The man started to cry. He put his right hand over his forehead and eyes to cover the torrent of tears. He was afraid of having something new. He didn't want anything to change. He wanted the channels added to his TV, but not a different way of changing channels. Ironically, the numbers on his remote were so faded that they were hardly legible.

I knelt down beside him and patted his arm with my hand and said, "Please, sir, don't cry. It's okay; what do you want me to do?"

"I want it back the way it was," he said between sniffles.

"I can do that, but you won't have the extra channels you wanted."

"I don't care anymore. I just want it back the way it was."

I said softly, "No problem. I will put it back the way it was."

After a few minutes, I turned around and said, "There, it's done. Here's your old remote." He received his old remote in his hand like a valued treasure.

"Sorry, I just don't understand all this new technology."

"It's okay." I stood up and patted him on the back.

As I left the small apartment, my trainee, Mike, said, "Man, I hope I never run into that!"

"Mike, that could be me in forty years. What goes around comes around."

My Day Got Fowled Up

As a courtesy, I usually try to call the customer ahead of time to let them know when to expect me.

I finish with an installation, and I punch in the next appointment on my GPS.

"Thirteen minutes to destination," it says.

I call the next customer. A man answers. "Hello."

"Hi, this is Dan from the cable company. According to my GPS, I will be arriving in thirteen minutes. I just wanted to make sure you were home."

The customer responds, "Do you know where I live?"

He doesn't see the *duh* on my face. "Yes. It's printed on the work order, and my GPS gave me directions."

There's a long pause. Finally, he says, "Well, we live on the right side of the road."

This conversation is already giving me an indication of what our face-to-face meeting could be like.

"Sir, I'm not sure how my GPS is bringing me there, so you may be on the left side of the road. Either way, I'll find you. I promise." I'm saying it with an assuring smile, but he can't see me. The silence on the other end of the line tells me he is slowly digesting what I said.

"We've always been on the right side of the road," he says.

"Okay. I'll see you thirteen minutes or so."

"Okay, see you soon. We'll be here!"

I hang up and shake my head. *What is this guy going to be like?*

Driving on a back road, I see a few cars ahead in both lanes with their brake lights on. As I pull up, I see the commotion. A flock of geese and goslings is meandering back and forth across the road. Drivers are honking their horns—as if the birds understand that a honking horn means *get off the road*. (Car honks and goose honks are different languages, you see.)

In the opposing lane, a woman gets out of her car and starts walking toward the geese, waving her arms around. She is trying to shoo the birds off the road, but they're just scattering.

I can clearly see that the birds have no respect for the kind-hearted woman. Both sides of the road are bordered by guardrails to keep vehicles from taking a dive into a creek on one side and a rocky gutter on the other.

I decide to get out and help, both to move the traffic along and to get me to my appointment.

I walk along the passenger side of the car in front of me so as not to frighten the flock back toward the woman. I move around the front of the car and join forces with her.

"Hi, thank you," she says, "I'm Betty. These geese seem like they're stuck and can't make up their minds."

I laugh. "With the two of us, Betty, we'll get them." Herding geese is a new experience for me. I've used my van to help herd some loose donkeys before, but never geese.

Between Betty and me, we move them along past my van.

My good deed completed, I get in, buckle up, and drive away. Betty waves as she passes me. I smile and mouth the words, 'Thank you!'

I'm now going to arrive later than I promised. Uh-oh. This customer might not be able to handle it.

I arrive twenty minutes after my phone call.

The man answers the door, and immediately I feel obligated to explain why I'm seven minutes later than I stated. "Sorry, I ran a bit late. I was helping someone on Orr Road. We were herding geese."

I say it with a smile, but his head pulls back and his double chin appears. "Why would you hurt geese? What did they ever do to you?"

I know my eyes have bugged out, because his head jerks back even more.

"No, no ... not *hurting* geese, *herding,* like a cowboy herding cattle."

His head settles back into neutral.

It turns out he *was* on the right side of the road, and he wasn't as strange as I thought. But I did learn something from this experience. When calling a customer to give an estimated time of arrival, add time!

With Friends Like Me . . .

I trained a guy named Mike Holland. He had a knack for being with me at the most opportune times to see me at my best, and he was an easy target for my pranks. We got into some pretty interesting situations, and when we chat on the phone every six months or so, we can't help but end up in stomach-busting laughter. After our recent phone conversation, I realized he deserved an entire chapter.

We were entering a house in the city. It was dark inside, even though it was early afternoon. The curtains were drawn, and the house was messy. We nearly ran into each other and tripped over things as we followed the customer up the steps.

As we found ourselves at the top of the stairs, the customer, who knew his way through his dungeon, was already in the room where we were heading.

Suddenly, we heard the noise.

It was a large dog, released from his cage in the bedroom. He was coming directly at us. All we could hear was the clinking of his chain collar and the pounding of his feet on the wood floor.

Mike and I were side by side when we first came around the corner in the hallway. Out of self-preservation, fear, and what *I* thought was common sense, I grabbed Mike by both of his shoulders and pulled him in front of me. (I'm laughing now as I write this, so much that there are tears in my eyes.)

Mike tried to step back, but it was too late. I was already

behind him, firmly gripping him as a shield and peering past his shoulder.

Mike later told me that he was shocked that I would use him to protect myself from the attacking animal. He said, "I couldn't see him, but I sure could hear him coming!"

As I was backing up, still clinging to Mike's winter coat, Mike yelled, "What are you doing?" I was afraid at that moment, but he was even more afraid. He was also mad at his boss for throwing him in the path of danger.

"I have children and you don't!" was my response.

Another two feet closer and the snarling beast would have had him, but Mike was saved by the customer grabbing the dog's chain and pulling him back into the dark chasm of his bedroom.

To this day, whenever Mike and I chat, that story makes us both laugh, and we have remained friends, despite my moment of cowardice.

Paint It Red

I'm not a fashion consultant or an interior designer, but I am in enough homes to tell what looks good and what doesn't. It took years for this talent to develop, so it's by no means an accident when I am asked for an opinion.

Often, when entering a home, I will see something rather stunning or eye-catching, and I have to comment.

"Wow, what a view from your back door. I bet you see a lot of deer, don't you?" It opens up a conversation without seeming too personal.

Perhaps the detailed marble floor in the foyer or an extraordinary painting will cause me to pause to admire it. The customer will see the effect it's having on me and say something.

The homes I have been in have been beautifully decorated, or horribly neglected, or just average, though being in a normal house is a rare occurrence.

I was installing cable in an apartment that had a double glass sliding door leading to a balcony. It was the end of summer and the door was open, with a screen door in place to keep the flies out. The customer threw her keys and purse on the dining room table as she led me into her apartment.

"Well, here it is. Home sweet home. It's not much, but it's what I have for now."

I nodded and moved toward the TV. "I've been here for a month and I just can't decide what do to with these awful curtains. Everything in here is so boring."

I looked up at the drapes drawn back from the double door. They were tan—and bland.

I said, "You know what you could do?" I began to offer a few suggestions. "It's summer now, and the lighter curtains reflect the light from outside. What you could do is use a different color for the sash, maybe a burgundy or royal green. Then, if you have permission from the management here, paint this wall a few tints darker, contrasting the wall where the door is. An accent wall can do wonders to make a room more attractive and not so boring."

She stared at me.

I continued. "In the winter, I would change the curtains to a darker color to match the accent wall, with the sash being the lighter color. By doing this, you create a warm space when it's cold outside."

Her mouth opened slowly and her eyes started moving toward the "accent" wall.

"What do you suggest?"

I now had her fully engaged in visualization. I walked over to the wall and pointed to the carpet. It was a dark brown. "See the floor's color? It's dark so as not to show dirt. This wall is off-white, but if you get some color samples from a paint store, you can hold them against the floor and get an idea of what colors would complement each other. A shade of green on this wall and the wall with the double doors could be a lot darker, making this room pop!"

I was excited, but her face was saying, *Who is this guy?*

I noted her expression and said, "Sorry. I was just trying to help."

She shook her head. "No, no. It's quite all right. I really like your ideas."

It was an invitation to drop some more of my incredible decorating ideas in her lap.

"You could also get a runner for your dining room table that matches the darker accent wall for the winter, and then a lighter one for the summer."

She looked back at the table where her keys and purse were

sitting. She was quiet for a moment. Then she said, "Could I hire you to do this?"

I laughed. "Nah, I'm just the cable guy. Where do you want your TV?"

Strong Stomach Required

A frail voice beckoned me into the apartment.

I opened the door slowly. Heavy curtains blocked all light, except for the light spilling in from the hallway. My shadow stretched into the small living room.

"Hi, I'm Dan. Here to install the cable."

"I'm over here." The voice was coming from a padded lounge chair. Then I saw the woman.

"Shut the door, please!" she said sternly.

I pulled the door closed and said, "I need to see where I'm going, ma'am. May I use my flashlight?"

There was a pause.

"Yes, but keep it pointed at the floor. I suffer from a skin disease, and I cannot handle too much light."

I felt bad for her. She was wearing sunglasses, and there was a dark, plastic film draped over the screen of the TV.

I saw what I needed and went outside to hook up her cable.

I didn't smell the odor until my return to the cave. My visual senses were dimmed, but my nose began to compensate. The odor wasn't normal. It smelled like something, a mouse perhaps, had crawled into her apartment and died.

I finished screwing the cable to the wall plate and then to the TV. Then I asked the customer if I could show her how the remote worked. She agreed, and I put one knee down on the carpet, leaned over the arm of the chair, and began my lesson.

The smell was becoming tolerable. I was getting used to it. As my eyes adjusted to the darkness, I noticed that the skin on her legs and arms was peeling. I began to see small, white specks all over the carpet and on the arm of the chair. It was dried skin. I was kneeling on it, and my arm was resting on the chair.

I finished my lesson, and she signed the work order. When I left the darkness of her apartment, I looked down to see bits of skin all over my pants, boots, and the right sleeve of my shirt. As sorry as I felt for her, she could have warned me that I'd be a magnet for those dead skin cells.

I was sick for the next hour.

Lesson learned: don't kneel down on someone's carpet unless you're wearing a hazmat suit!

A Moving Experience

I helped a woman move. Oh, it wasn't in my plans.

She is scheduled to have her cable disconnected at her mobile home and hooked up at a new apartment.

When my trainee and I arrive to turn the service off, I notice a lot of people there to help her move. I don't know if she is at this house or at her new place, which is my next stop.

Turns out, she's standing in the mobile home, directing her helpers.

"Hi, ma'am. I'm Dan, from the cable company. I'm here to disconnect the service here and then hook you up at your new place. I have a question for you."

She's frazzled, overwhelmed, and out of breath. "Yes, what's the question?"

"Well, I see your TV here, and I'm going over to your apartment to turn on the cable. I guess what I'm asking is ... how do you want to handle this? Do you want me to just go turn it on and you bring your TV over now? Or can you hook it up yourself later?"

She stares down at the TV stand that holds a digital box, a DVR, a VCR, and an RF modulator. It's a wiring mess.

"Oh, sonny, if I take those wires apart, I'd never get it back together right."

It's my trainee's second day, and he sees me do something I have never done in decades of doing cable.

"Tell you what, ma'am. My trainee and I will load your TV stand and all its equipment in my van and take it over there for you."

The trainee doesn't say a word. I'm glad, too, because I don't want him to question me. On the other hand, I don't want him to think this is normal.

"I have to go to another appointment first, but after that, I'll show up at your apartment and hook it all up. Is that okay?"

She looks relieved. "Oh, thank you! I'll go over now and unlock it for you, but I have to come back here right away."

I nod and give directions to my trainee as we load her stuff into my van. Thirty minutes later, we arrive at her new apartment.

Her son is walking out the door as we carry this load up a flight of steps.

"Oh, you're the cable guys!" he says. "My mom said you would be stopping by today, but I didn't know you were bringing her TV too! What service!"

I respond, "Please don't tell anyone I did this. I never do this. Honest!"

We set up all the wiring and give her a new remote.

As we leave, the trainee asks, "Is this normal?"

I say, "It was normal for this situation, but I've never done this before."

Before you think I'm a total saint, I have to admit there was some selfishness to my act of kindness. If I had waited for her movers take her TV over to the new place, I'd have been waiting a long time. It was a Saturday, and I wanted to get done early.

Anyway, it became a win-win situation. She got her TV hooked up with all the accessories, and I got done early.

And I'd do it again.

Falsely Accused

The house was huge. It sat on a quiet street, with neighbors an acre apart.

"Here to install your Internet."

The woman answered the door and took me upstairs. "The Internet is going in here. This is my husband's office."

Boxes were everywhere. They had just moved in, and the moving company had just left.

She disappeared down the hall and entered the master bedroom. I walked by and shouted, "Going outside, I'll be back in a few!" I heard a voice coming from somewhere within the maze of boxes. "Okay ... I'm lost in here somewhere."

I laughed and went down the steps and outside. I completed the install outside. Now all I had to do was connect the wire to the modem.

"Are you almost done?" she asked.

"Yes. Maybe ten more minutes and I'll have your computer up and running." She turned away and disappeared again into the cardboard maze.

The doorbell rang. She bounded down the steps to the front door and I heard, "Well, yes ... he is here. He's upstairs." I knew she had to be talking about me.

I heard footsteps coming in my direction, then a man's voice. "Dan?"

The voice was familiar, but only because I'd been talking to him just ninety minutes before. He was a neighbor who lived a few doors down. He was a retired police officer with a tough swagger, yet a kind voice. I had just installed his cable, and after seeing my van, he stopped by to pick up a few extra channel-guide cards.

I walked him out to my van and happily gave him what he wanted, and then went back to work.

A little while later, I was wrapping up this job. I raised my voice in a friendly tone. "Finished!"

She came into the room smiling and was happy to see the computer screen showing a website. "You did a fantastic job. Thanks so much. I just hope my husband will help me unpack instead of getting on this thing," she said, pointing to the computer. "He is going through withdrawal!"

I handed her the clipboard and a pen. She signed the form and I left.

Two hours later, the local dispatch lady called me on my cell. She had the personality of a skittish goat: turn your back and she'd ram you.

"Dan, did you take something from an installation?" Keep in mind, when you are entering as many houses as I do in a year's time, you have to have a squeaky-clean reputation. If you didn't, you wouldn't be working long.

"Of course not, Cathy," I said.

"Well, you need to call Mr. Smith. He is very angry at you. Here's his number."

I must admit, I was offended that she would even *ask* a question like that, but then again, I don't think she trusted anyone.

"Okay, I'll call him." I pulled over and made the call.

He answered the phone in a professional way. "Hello?"

"Hi, this is Dan. I understand you wanted me to call. Something is missing?"

His voice immediately turned dark with jagged anger. "I don't know what you're trying to pull here, buddy, but you stole my GPS, and I want it back!"

I paused. "Sir, I didn't take your GPS. If there were a quarter lying on your sidewalk, I wouldn't pick it up, because it's not mine."

He didn't like the comparison, as evidenced by his retort. "Listen, Dan," he said with an indignant tone, "this is not a coin. This is an eight-hundred-dollar GPS unit, and I want it back."

He was intent on my confessing. "I don't have it to give it back," I said.

He stepped up his attack; his voice reached a new pitch. I could almost feel the redness filling his face as his blood pressure rose. "My wife told me that *you* were the *only* person in the house today and *you* are the *only* one who could have taken it!"

"Sir, there was another man in the house. He was a neighbor who stopped by. I can have him call you. I have his phone number."

The silence of a few seconds was broken by a fervent accusation. "Now *you* are calling *my* wife a *liar!*"

Now I was done with being nice. "Mr. Smith, I can verify that another person entered the house by a simple phone call—"

He interrupted me. "I'm calling the police. You either drop it off on my front porch with no questions asked *or* I'll call the police."

I responded slowly, drawing out the words. "I do not have your GPS. You can call the police. And by the way, the neighbor who stopped in is a retired police officer."

Pause. "I'm pressing charges," he said. "You better get a good lawyer!" With that, he hung up.

My heart was pounding. *What do I do?* I went to the local sheriff's office and explained my quandary. The officer at the desk told me that the burden of proof was on the customer. If he didn't see me take it, it's my word against his.

The day was over. I was a wreck. At seven o'clock that night, my cell phone rang. It was the angry customer's number. I let it go to voice mail. I took a few breaths and then dialed my voice mail.

"Dan, this is Mr. Smith. I need to apologize. I found the GPS. My wife must have knocked it over when we were moving boxes. It showed up when we were unpacking."

I shook my head. How quickly he accused me without a shred of evidence. My reputation was now at stake with the cable company.

The stress I dealt with, thinking, *What's going to happen?* I tossed and turned all night, even though I was innocent.

The next morning, I pulled into the cable company parking lot. A state trooper was sitting in his car. I nodded as I walked past him and opened the door to the office.

"Why is he here?" I asked the receptionist. Not knowing her joke would bother me, she said, "Oh, he's probably here for *you!*"

The trooper walked in and announced, "I'm looking for Dan Armstrong."

My heart sank. "I'm Dan Armstrong."

He flipped open a small, black notebook. "I have to ask you a few questions."

I reached for my cell phone. "Wait! Is this about a GPS unit?"

He cocked his head back. "Yeah ..."

I flipped open my phone and said, "Hold on. Let me play you a voice mail." I was so glad I had saved it!

He listened to the message, closed his notebook, and as it snapped shut, he said, "Well, *they* forgot to call us."

He left, and I promptly called my lawyer. I wanted him to demand that the customer write an apology letter, including an admission that he had falsely accused me.

A week later, the letter was on file, and my job was safe. Whew!

Just to Be Clear

Some people need absolute clarity when being asked a question.

"Sir, where would like your cable?"

He looks at me and says, "Duh! On the TV!"

I nod. "Okay, I get it. Where are your TVs that need cable?"

He shows me, shaking his head in an obvious way to indicate to me how stupid I am.

"Sir, where is your basement?"

He shakes his head again and says in a demeaning tone, "It's downstairs."

I say, "Okay, it's downstairs. What I should have asked you is, 'Where is the door to your basement?' Right? Is that how you want me to ask questions?"

His lips pucker out, and his eyebrows scrunch together. "You can ask them any #@*% way you want."

I pucker my mouth in imitation and scowl back, but in a kinder way. "Well, sir, I'm here by your invitation. I want to do a good job, and I ask a lot of questions because I want you to be happy when I leave. Does that make sense?" He seems to get it, I think.

"So, how long have you been doing cable?" he asks.

I cannot help myself. I want to bite my tongue, but my mouth races ahead of me. "How long have I been doing cable? Do you mean as a profession, or here in your house? Could you be more clear?"

Are You *Kidding* Me?

I knocked on the door of an upstairs apartment. I was there to pick up equipment.

After quite awhile, an elderly woman opened the door.

She was out of breath. "I was shouting for you to come in," she said.

I felt so bad. "Ma'am, I did not hear you at all. I am so sorry you had to come down all those stairs. I would have called, but your number is dead."

"Oh, that's all right," she said as she began the climb back up the steps. I apologized again. About three-quarters of the way up, she stopped to take a few breaths.

"Oh, ma'am, I am truly sorry. I sure wish I could have heard you."

She turned to me. "Oh, it's okay ... I can't hardly shout anymore ... bad lungs ... we're almost at the top."

She looked up and grasped the handrail to climb the last few steps.

We made it to the top, and I guess I really felt bad, because I said it again.

"I really do feel bad ..." And that's when my sentence trailed off.

There on the couch was young man, around twenty-five years old, wrapped in a blanket.

I looked at him with a smirk and said—loudly, "Or I guess, ma'am, your grandson could have come down and let me in."

His response? "Dude, I'm playing a game."

Seething, I said under my breath, "You might be playing a game, but the rest of us are living in the real world."

Of course, he didn't hear me. He was focused on the "important" task at hand.

Some people's grandkids!

My First Old Folks' Home

I am twenty years old and entering a world I have never seen before.

As I walk in, she is staring at the ceiling above her bed. The room is small, and the odor is trapped in the space she now calls home.

"They're gone. They're all gone." She speaks, still gazing upward. Glancing up at the drop ceiling and then back at her, I say, "Hi, I'm Dan. I'm here to hook up your TV."

I say it in a gentle way. I find myself speaking to the elderly who live in nursing homes the same way I speak to little children when I, this stranger, enter their homes.

Checking in at the front desk at many of these homes is normal protocol. Show your badge to identify yourself, and then present the work order to validate your visit.

The front-desk lady says, "Oh, hi! Good, I'm glad you're here. Ms. Sadie has been here a week with no TV. She's a big Phillies fan, and she is going nuts." It's kind of surprising to me that an elderly lady would be such a sports fan. I always assumed it would be "man" thing.

I am escorted down the halls, walking past wheelchair-bound people, some of them sagging over but strapped in tight. An old woman with short-cropped gray hair reaches out for me. "Take me home ..."

This is my first experience installing cable at an "old folks' home." The ceilings are low. The long, narrow hallway has the same old-style linoleum squares as my elementary school, and the smell reminds me of that horrific stench from when some kid threw up his lunch.

"Here we are," my tour guide announces. "Ms. Sadie, the cable man is here."

I walk into the cramped room. It has a bed, a dresser, and a nightstand with a lamp and a TV. I'm wondering how she rolls in here and gets into the bed. "They're gone; they're all gone ..."

I introduce myself and begin connecting the TV. "They're gone," she drones, and then she sees me as I move the TV back to the wall.

"Look at this place." She is speaking intelligently. "I lived in a farmhouse, and now look." She wants me to look at the room. There's a Phillies pendant on the wall beside her bed, a picture of her with a man—must be her husband—and a pile of cards on her nightstand. "This is what I'm reduced to."

I am new to this idea that a customer would tell her life story to a complete stranger. "I was married to George for fifty-four years. We had three children—two boys and a girl." She's looking at the picture. "We had a wonderful life, and then he died."

She tears up and wipes her nose with a cloth hanky she holds in her hand.

She begins telling me her story. "My daughter died in 1972, and my son, George Jr., died after an operation on his heart."

As she is describing the years that have passed, I begin to understand why she is telling me all of this. She wants me to know that this is *not* who she is. She makes very clear the heartache of living in this small room as compared to the farmhouse where she became a housewife, raised her children, tended a garden, and lost her husband and two of her children. Without saying it directly, she wants me to know that she didn't plan this.

I am uncomfortable. It's hot. I want to leave now.

The TV finally warms up. I find her remote on the nightstand and give it to her.

She looks up at me, the look in her eyes saying, *Don't go. Stay here and visit with me.* She can't sign the paperwork because her hands are practically molded around the remote.

"Have a good day," I say as I leave the room.

I find my way through the halls to the lobby, passing men and women bent with age, shuffling to who knows where. I look into their faces. I'm twenty. They are fifty, sixty, seventy years older than me. They've lived the span of my lifetime over and over.

A sweeping sense of awe strikes me. These people *were* twenty years old. Then they were twenty-eight, forty-four, fifty-one, and sixty-nine. Now they are dying in a strange building, with people they never knew their entire lives.

I am sick with emotion.

As this is in my early days of installing cable, every day holds a new adventure to absorb. But today is not an adventure.

Today is a lesson.

I Wouldn't Want That Job, Either

A customer was downgrading his cable service, so I was there to remove a large box and install a cheaper model.

He said he'd lost his job as a supervisor at a military base nearby. He'd asked his boss if he could take a pay cut and work at a lower pay grade. But, he explained, "I didn't want to deal with dead bodies."

Pause.

"Dead bodies?" I said. "Why would you work with dead bodies?"

"You know there are some people who donate their bodies to science. Well, we take them, inject them with a chemical to keep them from getting stiff, and then we put them in Humvees and blow them up."

"Why would you blow them up?"

"So we know how to build a better Hummer for the military. You have no idea what else we've done."

I looked down at the remote I was programming. "You've told me more than I wanted to know."

Meeting People

I'm amazed at how open people are with me after just meeting me at their front door.

Only a few minutes will pass, and life stories begin to pour out.

"We just moved in ... we lost our son at our old house, and it was just too much to stay there ..."

"My daughter's moving back in because her husband left her and she needs a place to stay ..."

"I'm moving in because my grandkids lost their dad last month. He was in Iraq ..."

They *could* just say, "Put the cable here."

But for some reason, without trying, I draw out a deeper reason for the call.

I look at them and pause, listen and purse my lips. "So sorry ..." Pause. "Is there a basement or utility room I need to see?"

Back to business, I try to move efficiently and professionally, but I do get emotionally pulled into their stories, the kinds of stories that their priest, pastor, or psychiatrist would hear. Tales of woe, stories of real life, exposed to a complete stranger.

When I leave, it's often with a fresh cup of coffee or a can of soda, or cookies soft out of the oven. New friends.

Saw a young man a few days ago at a gas station. "Dan!" he hollers.

I don't recognize him. "Yes?"

He walks over. "My wife had her baby! It was a girl!"

Suddenly, I get a glimpse of our short history. "Oh, yes. You live in the valley! The rancher, framed-out basement, hardwood floors, and a nippy dog."

He laughs. "That's right. Well, she was ready to pop that day, and she was just so happy to

have the cable on now that the baby is here."

Nodding, I reply, "Congratulations! Enjoy every day. They sure grow up fast!"

And then there's the guy I installed for ten years ago.

Once in a while, I see him in the parking lot of the Wawa store. He lives in Pennsylvania but drives to Maryland for a cup of coffee and a paper. I always stop at his pickup truck window and chat for a few minutes. We know each other's names.

A passerby would think we're old friends catching up (which is what we're doing), but what it comes down to is, one day, I installed his cable.

I'm Not the Guy You're Looking For

I get the work order and don't think anything of the last name until I enter the house and say, "Hi, I'm Dan. Here to install your cable. Are you Jim Kable?"

He says, "Yes. And you pronounced it right. It sounds just like *cable*."

A quick nod from me. "So it does. That's interesting."

He takes me to the rooms where he wants the cable.

I get busy, and an hour later, I'm done. He signs the paperwork. I go out to my van, which is parked in the driveway, and start the engine.

A police car pulls in behind me and flashes his lights.

I'm thinking, *I'm not even driving. What did I do? My inspection is current. I'm not parked illegally. Hmmm ...*

The two police officers get out of their car. I look in my rear-view mirror as the one makes a wide berth to the right of my van. He is walking slowly up the grade of the yard. A slight hill gives him a distinct advantage.

The other officer, who was the driver, is walking directly alongside my van with his right hand up, a signal not to move.

I begin to roll down my window. Peripheral vision allows me to see the officer to my right immediately pause. He saw me moving.

The one coming up in direct sight of my driver-side mirror says, "Don't move." He is six feet behind me.

I slowly raise my hands off the steering wheel and put them

in plain sight over the open window. The officer on my side says, "Turn off the engine."

I reach back with my right hand and turn the key, keeping my left hand still. There is a strange quiet, as if the birds are all watching with bated breath.

My nerves are making my arms quiver. I fill my lungs with a slow, deliberate draw. I feel as though I am watching this happen instead of experiencing it.

Then I speak up. "What's going on, sir?"

The driver-side officer asks in a very authoritative tone, "Are you Kable?"

Of course, my immediate thought is that *I am!*

Then the past hour of activity flashes in my mind. *Wait a minute ... they're not saying* cable*, they're saying* Kable. My mind races for the right words. I still remember what I said. "I am the *cable man*, but I'm not the *man, Kable,* you are looking for."

The cop to the right is now directly at my passenger-side window, looking back into my cargo area. It's becoming obvious that I really am a cable guy.

I ask, "I guess he's in some kind of trouble, but would you mind backing up so I can leave? I have a real busy day."

The cop on the right walks toward the house while the other backs out and parks on the street. I back out and wave as I drive away.

Looks like Mr. Kable won't be able to watch cable tonight.

Dude, That's Not Normal

I followed the man as he led me to the second-floor bedroom where he wanted a TV connected to cable.

The odor of stale urine was strong. I lifted my T-shirt at the collar to cover my nose and mouth. Beside the bed was a large container of dark-yellow urine. The carpet was spotted all around the bucket where he had missed or drizzled. It was truly a disgusting sight and smell.

"Sir, could you remove *that?*" I pointed to the offending substance beside his bed.

"Sure," he said as he bent over to pick it up. There were no handles, so both his hands were employed as he gently lifted the poison. I backed up as far as I could. My eyes must have been bugging out at the sight of it—and from the chance that the bucket would slip from his grasp.

The bathroom was only ten feet away, one door down, yet he chose to sit on his bed and do his business this way.

It took him three flushes to get rid of his urine, and then he brought the container back and placed it at the same spot.

"I don't like to get up at night to pee, so it's just easier to do it in the bucket." He was no older than twenty-five and had no physical handicaps that would prevent him from walking ten feet to use the toilet.

"You can't walk to the bathroom to pee?" I asked boldly.

"I could, but I'm usually drunker than a skunk." He laughed. I didn't.

I said, "I didn't know skunks got drunk."

He paused to reflect as I began to drill.

"I guess this isn't normal, is it?" he asked.

"No, dude, it's not normal."

After I left his house, I sprayed the bottom of my boots with Lysol and removed them before I went into my house at the end of the day.

Scenes like these stick to the memory like bubble gum to hair. I just hoped that whatever I walked through didn't stick as long.

Heartbreaking

Many years ago, I walked up to the front door of a ramshackle house. Spiderwebs hung in front of the door. Shrubbery clung to the crumbling mortar and grappled its way up to the second-floor windows.

Tires and rusted metal lay strewn throughout the yard. A broken wheelbarrow tilted precariously near the front door. The grass had gotten so high, it had given up and fallen over.

It was like walking onto a Halloween display. Black sheets covered the windows. No lights that I could see.

I knocked. A hollow-faced man opened the door, which creaked in two discordant tones. The door wouldn't open fully, blocked on the inside by piles of trash that never made it to the curb.

His face was craggy, his clothing dirty. He was shoeless, and his toenails were black.

"Come in. Here to hook me up, huh?"

I was a bit cautious as I entered. It was obvious he had not opened this door—or any door—to leave for quite some time.

"Yeah," I said. "You want two TVs connected?"

He rubbed his stubbled chin as he thought. "Yeah, I guess. My sister is paying for this."

It was cold in the house. Even for a fall day, it was warmer outside.

We walked into the living room to sights that are hard to imagine: papers, piles of magazines, trash, opened cans of food carelessly tossed about. Silverware crusted with dried food lay everywhere on the floor.

The carpet was brown, but the edges showed evidence that the original color was a soft olive green.

I thought I'd seen the worst until I walked into his bedroom.

There was his bed, with the blankets pushed to the bottom. On the filthy sheets, I noticed the black outline of his body, much like what you might see at a crime scene. He didn't bathe. He didn't clean himself, his clothing, or the house. The sheets absorbed his grime every night as he lay down.

Drinking glasses held mysterious liquids topped with a green paste. The mold was thick, and it was everywhere.

The smell was repulsive, but I breathed through my nose so I couldn't taste it. Even shallow draws of air made it feel like dust and stale food were coating my lungs.

"I'll be right back. I need to get my tools."

I was angry. I really was. How could anyone live like this—live in such filth? *Get a garbage bag, dude, and clean this place up!* I wanted to say.

An hour later, I was done. He was sitting on his lounge chair dozing off, his hand on the side of his head.

"Sir, I'm finished," I said, startling him.

He took a look at the TV in front of him, which was now showing the news. "It's fuzzy," he said.

I walked over to the TV, picked a T-shirt off the floor, and began to wipe the black soot from the screen. It clung to the cloth as small, blue sparks of static electricity tapped the screen.

"How's that look?" I asked.

He leaned forward from his chair and stared intently. "That looks good."

I put an *X* where he needed to sign the paperwork. "Can you sign this?" I handed him the clipboard and my pen, not wanting to retrieve the pen after he handled it.

I looked down at his hands as he began to write. He was slow and deliberate, shaking as he studied each letter. His torn, ragged, brown sweater was stained with dried spaghetti sauce—perhaps last night's dinner—from where he had wiped his hands.

Then he spoke.

"Sorry about the mess. I am very sick. I was in Vietnam and got sprayed with Agent Orange. My whole body aches, my eyes are bad, I can't concentrate. I've gotten worse. I don't have long, and my sister wanted me to have some sort of entertainment."

My throat tightened up. I couldn't speak. My eyes began to well with tears. My jaw dropped and my heart pounded.

Then my heart broke.

The only thing I could think to say was, "May I pray for you?"

He handed me the clipboard and said, "That would be okay with me."

I laid the clipboard on the table beside me and placed my hand on the spot of dried spaghetti sauce. I didn't even feel it.

"God ... I don't know this man, but you do. You know his heart, and you know what he needs. God, would you meet him here today and meet his every need for the time he has left here on earth?"

I barely got it out.

He sniffed at the same time I did. Then he reached up and shook my hand.

As I drove away, I began to weep. "Oh, God, how could I be so judgmental! I didn't know the story of that man."

It taught me a very valuable lesson.

It was a small cable company in Chester County, so I was often in the office several times during the day.

A woman walked in carrying a bag with some cable equipment in it. "I am returning these," she said. "I need to cancel the service for my brother. He died."

I stood up from the cubicle and came around to offer my sympathies. "I am sorry for your loss. What was the address of your brother?"

As she said it, it felt like a roll of thunder was vibrating on my chest.

"Your brother died? I am so sorry. I met him ... I mean, I ... I installed his cable."

She drew back and said, "Thank you. He told me that the guy that came out was kind enough to pray for him. I am so grateful for that. Thank you."

My mind goes blank after that. I don't remember what I said or when she left the office.

I do remember thinking that I might have been the last person he saw.

The Detective

Most of my customers who are police officers do not flaunt their profession. In fact, they typically don't even bring it up during my visit in their home.

Often, my discovery of their vocation is by accident. I have to run a wire through a closet. Sliding their uniforms across the bar, I see the neatly pressed shirts and jackets with the insignia stitched into the fabric.

Sometimes, the obvious clue is a sheriff's-deputy car or state police car in the driveway.

At times, it's the haircut, their build, or just the way they answer the door or the way they walk that shows their confident authority.

Reading someone as they open the door is a skill I've acquired over decades of meeting strangers, especially in their homes, the place where they are most comfortable.

This man answered the door with a gallop and a fast forward handshake. He greeted me like I was an old friend, slapping me on the back as I entered. I felt welcome immediately.

"Would you like some coffee?" he asked with a broad smile. He towered over me and looked like he could have been a college basketball coach. "Black? Or do you want cream and sugar?"

I was surprised by his hospitality from the moment I walked in. "Black, please," I responded and then got to work.

Throughout the time I was there, I kept noticing his T-shirt.

The front bore a circle just above the heart that read "Baltimore City Homicide Department."

"I see you're a police officer?" I asked respectfully.

"Yes. Well, I was. I just retired."

I nodded. "You were in homicide? I bet that was a challenge, huh?"

His body language shifted and his smile disappeared for a moment. He paused and stared into the distance, perhaps remembering a grisly scene.

"Yeah, I had a lot of bad days and a lot of bad nightmares." Then his smile returned. "But that's in the past, and I don't look back."

Maybe I shouldn't have said anything, I thought.

When he turned to get his checkbook, I saw the back of his T-shirt. I had to read it several times to make sure I'd read it right.

As he turned to face me, he saw my focused stare. He gestured over his shoulder. "You like that, huh?"

"Yeah! I love it!"

He laughed and said, "I got another one! Do you want it?"

I must have looked like a little kid who's just been offered his favorite candy. "Are you serious? I would love one!"

He left the room and returned shortly with a gray T-shirt. Just like the one he was wearing, the front read "Baltimore City Homicide Department."

The back: "Our Day Begins When Your Day Ends."

Hidden Treasures

Walking out of the Wawa store in Nottingham, Pennsylvania with my hot, black coffee, I see the flash of green on the concrete just outside the door. It's a five-dollar bill folded in half.

I figure it had to have fallen out of the pocket of the person right in front of me.

I swoop down like a hawk on a field mouse and look ahead of me. "Sir! Sir!"

The man is moving toward the gas pumps. I am now within a few feet of him. "Did you lose a five-dollar bill?"

He turns and says, "Maybe, I'll have to check," and begins to dig in his pockets.

I am already handing him the Lincoln. "Here, it's not mine anyway."

He takes it and thanks me, and I keep walking.

But ... it might *not* have been his. Only a minute later, I'm thinking, *I could have used that!*

Oh, well. It reminded me of an installation some years ago.

I was a wall fisher. That means that the customer wanted an outlet in the wall fished down from the attic or up from the basement.

I arrived at a large house and a woman answered the door. "Come on in. I'll show you where we want the outlet."

We went to the second floor and she showed me the room. I

tapped on the wall to find a hollow spot, then asked to see the access to the attic.

"Here it is." She pointed to a square of removable drywall in her office.

After setting up my stepladder, I crawled through the opening.

A moment later, I was in the dark attic. Typically, attics do not have floorboards to walk on, but this one did. That's not a good thing, because it hides the wall studs below, and I can't see the room outline when I pull away the insulation. I did my measurements and found where the wall should be.

I reached under the floorboards, and I felt something.

My hands wrapped around a cylindrical container. Carefully, I slid the find out from under the floorboard and set it under the solitary light bulb hanging from the rafters.

The container was heavy, but I had to move it because of where I needed to drill. I drilled the hole and pushed the wire down, then turned back to the container.

What could possibly be in there that would weigh so much? Do I open it? Should I just put it back where I found it and forget about it?

I decided to open it.

My eyes bugged out! Gold and silver coins—lots of them. Below a few coins, wrapped in plastic, was a piece of yellow paper folded several times. I wanted to unfold it, read it, and return the treasure where I found it.

I squirmed my way down the hatch into the office.

She was sitting at her desk. "Uh, ma'am ..." I was not sure how to tell her. "I found a lot of money in your attic. Do you want me to leave it there or bring it down?"

She seemed surprised, yet skeptical. "Oh, sure, bring it down!" *She doesn't believe me.*

"No, seriously, there is a tub of money up there. I didn't know if maybe you forgot about it or whatever."

She stood up from her cluttered desk. "You are serious."

I responded with a smile. "Yes. I'll get it for you."

Minutes later, I presented her with something that held a twenty-five-year-old mystery that was about to be solved.

After I showed her the bucket of money, she immediately got on the phone. I could hear her frantically chasing her husband down at the office. After leaving messages with different departments, she hung up, visibly shaken.

I finished my work, took all my tools out to my van, and then came back in the house to get her signature on the work order.

When I entered the house, I heard her voice in high shrills. She was crying. I made my presence known by walking slowly into the room and clearing my throat.

"Are you okay?" I asked, careful not to sound too personal. She turned toward me. There were tears on her cheeks.

"This was my father's doing," she said. "This was a gift from him. He told us twenty-five years ago when we built the house that he put a housewarming present in the house for us. We never found it. We thought he was joking, and he never revealed it to us. And we didn't think to ask him when he was dying. He's gone now, but today I feel like I am seeing my father again. This letter is his handwriting. Every coin is listed here. Every coin!"

She started to whimper. I was not sure what to say. "Ma'am, I'm sorry—"

She interrupted me. "No, don't be sorry; you found something that we would have *never* found. Thank you."

I nodded. "Would you do me a favor?" I asked.

"Yes," she said immediately.

I didn't think it was unreasonable, and being curious, I wanted to know.

"When you count this or get it appraised, would you call me and let me know how much this bucket of money is worth?"

She smiled. "Of course."

Some time passed, and then I got the call.

Seven thousand dollars.

Alone in the Dungeon of Mystery

The old, white two-story farmhouse was in need of repair. The loose gravel driveway was edged by dirt flattened by the tires of his pickup.

As I swept into his driveway behind the blue truck, he stepped out of the house onto the wood deck by the side door.

"How ya doing?" he called out in a friendly way.

"I'm good. Here to install your cable."

He smiled broadly. "Great! Been waiting for this day!"

He opened the screen door and we walked in, allowing it to slam closed in a country way.

He pointed to my patient. "Well, there's the TV!"

"Any cable wire behind that?" I asked.

"Nope. The people that lived here before never had cable. This house is over a hundred years old and barely has enough electrical outlets. And *no* closets! But I love it!"

I nodded with a smile. "I love these old houses," I said.

I pulled the TV cart from the wall and saw a hole through the floor.

"I can run my wire down through that hole, if that's all right with you."

He glanced behind the TV. "Yeah, that's fine. I'll show you the basement." We walked over worn linoleum floors and into the kitchen, where he opened an old, wooden door with flaking paint on both sides.

He said, "There's no light down there, so I hope you have a flashlight."

I reached into my cargo pants pocket and produced a small flashlight. "Always have it with me!"

The steps creaked under our weight as we descended into the darkness. I surveyed the basement and saw a window on the other end that leaked sunlight through layers of dirt.

I reached down and grabbed a piece of wood to begin clearing a path through the drooping, dust-laden cobwebs.

Then we heard a noise behind us.

"What was that?" I asked at once.

He turned and looked. My flashlight scanned the black corners.

Quietly, he said, "I've heard noises down here before, but I'm assuming it's just the old wood creaking under my feet."

I threw the beam of light around the dirt floor and saw old cardboard boxes sitting on a wooden pallet. "I don't see anything," I said.

I moved toward the window to see where I could bring the cable in from the outside. That's when I saw something.

"Sir? Could you come over here?"

He shuffled in the darkness toward me.

I pointed the flashlight at the wood trim around the window. There were scratch marks on it.

He looked at it and said, "I think the neighbor's cat is trying to get in here to get mice."

I said, "No, these scratch marks are on the *inside*." I paused. "I think something is trying to get *out!*"

We heard the noise again, and the man took off up the stairs. The door at the top of the steps slammed, leaving me alone in the dungeon of mystery.

Then I heard it again.

I aimed my flashlight in the direction of the sound. I saw a movement of fur and two beady eyes glowing red.

Chills crept up my neck.

Then it appeared again as it ran from one box to another. It looked like a huge rat.

When I saw the tail, I figured it out. It was an opossum.

I calmly walked up the steps and discovered that, in his haste, the man had slammed the door so hard I had to shove it open with my shoulder.

I walked out the screen door and saw him standing at the back of his truck.

He looked up at me and said, "Sorry, dude! That scared the heck out of me! What's down there?"

I laughed and told him, "It's an opossum. It probably got in somewhere around the foundation."

I went ahead and did my work, keeping the flashlight in my mouth as I stapled the wire to the basement ceiling beams. I didn't hear the critter again.

"You should probably call the local wildlife service," I told the customer, "and they can get it out for you."

He was visibly shaken. "Can that thing come upstairs?"

I chuckled again. "No, it doesn't have opposable thumbs like we do, so it can't turn your doorknob." But I was thinking, *No, dude! It's too short to reach the doorknob, so it can't open it, walk up the stairs to your second floor, and crawl in bed with you.*

But I figured that mental picture would have been too much for him.

"They're Shooting at Us!"

It's another day of training for Mike Holland.

We are going to a house that is on the same road as a police firing range. It's an odd thing to hear gunfire so close to houses, but they are safely up the road and firing into a solid, forty-foot-high dirt cliff.

I have this information before we go to the neighborhood, and this can only mean one thing: I'm going to get Mike real good!

As I get out of the van, I say to Mike, "Now, I have to let you know that this is a *really* bad area. Always lock your truck, always walk slowly to the house, and read your work order as you approach the house. That way when the customer looks outside, you don't seem to be a threat."

His eyes widen.

"I want you to know everything I do so you're safe." I keep building up this story, and I'm hoping the firing range is in session.

We enter the house and introduce ourselves. I say to the customer, "We have to go outside and hook you up at the pole, and then we'll be back."

Mike is walking up the steps toward the street when suddenly, we hear the sound. *Blap! Blap! Blap-blap-blap!*

I shout, "Mike, they're shooting at us! Get down!" Mike turns his head left to right in a flash and drops at the same time, slapping his chest on the sidewalk. His arms are lying flat on either side of his head, and he is practically kissing the concrete.

Of course, I start howling.

Not sure what to think and still on his belly, Mike lifts his head and says, "What's going on?"

Blap-blap! Blap-blap-blap-blap! The shots ring out again. Mike throws his hands on the back of his head. I am now in disbelief at the timing of the police firing and our presence at that moment. I could not have planned this any better! Tears have now reached my cheek, and Mike begins to realize that my laughter is directed at him.

"You jerk!" Mike stands to his feet and brushes off the dust. He is also looking around to see if anyone saw him drop. He yells at me, "You scared me!"

I am trying to speak through coughs and laughter. "Oh man ... you should ... have seen ... your face!"

Mike is clearly not amused.

Not long after that, Mike was training someone and did the exact same prank. Even though I wasn't there for that one, I know Mike would have made me proud.

Conclusion

Normal is a relative term, and I don't mean your family members or mine.

We live in a quirky world with quirky people. Entering into the home of a complete stranger carries responsibility and requires common sense.

The customer's response to you is totally unpredictable. Learning how to adapt has been an adventure in itself. Despite how a home might look or smell, and despite how customers might treat you, treating the person and their domain with respect can go a long way toward building that instant rapport you need.

I hope you have enjoyed reading *The Adventures of a Real-Life Cable Guy.* As I wrote these stories, many other experiences came flooding to my mind. I would find myself scrambling for a notepad, an envelope, or a store receipt, and writing a few words to jar my memory later.

Unfortunately, by the time I retrieved the scribbles, I couldn't always decipher what I meant. *What was I thinking when I wrote this?* It was like waking up at two a.m. and writing in the dark.

And then there are the many stories that I just have not had time to write.

So I haven't finished writing yet. Meeting five to ten people per day means the chances are pretty good that I'll have many more stories to tell. Perhaps there will be a second book, called *More Adventures of a Real-Life Cable Guy.*

Stay tuned.